W9-ALJ-538

your

enthusiasm

WRITTEN BY
DEIRDRE DOLAN

DESIGNED BY
PH.D

PRODUCED BY

MELCHER
MEDIA

PUBLISHED BY

GOTHAM
BOOKS

IT'S NOT TV. IT'S HBO

curb your enthusiasm

The Book

Produced by Melcher Media

GOTHAM, Published by Penguin Group (USA) Inc., 375 Hudson Street, New York, New York 10014,
U.S.A.

Penguin Group (Canada), 90 Eglinton Avenue East, Suite 700, Toronto, Ontario M4P 2Y3, Canada (a
division of Pearson Penguin Canada Inc.); Penguin Books Ltd, 80 Strand, London WC2R 0RL, England;
Penguin Ireland, 25 St Stephen's Green, Dublin 2, Ireland (a division of Penguin Books Ltd); Penguin
Group (Australia), 250 Camberwell Road, Camberwell, Victoria 3124, Australia (a division of Pearson
Australia Group Pty Ltd); Penguin Books India Pvt Ltd, 11 Community Centre, Panchsheel Park, New
Delhi - 110 017, India; Penguin Group (NZ), cnr Airborne and Rosedale Roads, Albany, Auckland
1310, New Zealand (a division of Pearson New Zealand Ltd); Penguin Books (South Africa) (Pty) Ltd,
24 Sturdee Avenue, Rosebank, Johannesburg 2196, South Africa

Penguin Books Ltd, Registered Offices: 80 Strand, London WC2R 0RL, England

Published by Gotham Books, a member of Penguin Group (USA) Inc.

First printing, October 2006
10 9 8 7 6 5 4 3 2 1

Gotham Books and the skyscraper logo are trademarks of Penguin Group (USA) Inc.
ISBN 1-592-40230-5

PRINTED IN CHINA

CONTENTS

"I remember one time I asked Larry, 'Did you get into any confrontations today?' And he said, 'I have not gotten in one in two weeks, my friend!' And then I could almost see his mind clicking: 'Okay. Today I had a little problem.'"

BILL SCHEFT, COMEDY WRITER AND FORMER STANDUP

INTRODUCTION

Bring up Larry David's name and the first thing everyone wants to know is: "Is he really like that?" Does he really go through life picking fights with guys in wheelchairs, lesbian receptionists, his father-in-law?

Ask him directly, and he'll tell you he's playing a version of himself—a flashback to his days as a barely successful standup full of unbridled hostility in New York. It's a version of himself America fell in love with once before, through his alter-ego, George Costanza, on *Seinfeld*. But where shallowness, cowardice, and self-indulgence were easy to find lovable in a well-polished, joke-filled sitcom, in *Curb Your Enthusiasm* it's a little less easy. Where *Seinfeld* let us off the hook, *Curb* leaves us hanging. Larry David lets us peek behind the curtain and get a glimpse of our unvarnished selves, and, warts and all, we like what we see.

Curb reflects a side of ourselves we've never seen reflected on television—the real side. The side we're ashamed of and try to hide; the side that wants to drive illegally in the carpool lane, sneak into the best seat in the house, get something for nothing. Facing our inner liars and cheaters and masturbators each week, without the balm of punch lines and laugh tracks and cutesy slap-bass musical cues, feels more like life.

"I think people respond because I'm putting myself in very identifiable situations that happen to people a lot," says David. "When we were doing *Seinfeld*, I realized that there was this whole world available that nobody was writing about. And I didn't understand it. I mean it puzzled me. What's the big deal? It just wasn't being done. And I'm not being immodest when I say that. I just didn't see anything being done like *Seinfeld*. And that's why people took to it."

The difference between Larry David on *Curb* and Jerry Seinfeld on *Seinfeld* is that even during *Seinfeld*'s cultural reign, no one particularly cared if Jerry was "really like that." There was nothing dangerous about Jerry's charming indifference. People ask if Larry David is "really like that" because they want the answer to be yes. They might not have the spine to tell their friend's wife she's being lame, or get in a fight with a trick-or-treater, or go at it with a nine-year-old, but watching David do it every Sunday night is irresistible wish fulfillment, and the next best thing.

Larry David says success has made him more censorious than he used to be. He doesn't feel the kind of rage that every so often made him want to pick up a barstool and throw it across the room: "I've dropped one or two of the seven deadly sins," he says. David wouldn't go so far as to describe himself as happy, but he might be willing to admit that, if he's not, at least his anger is working for him.

Lawrence Gene David was born on a hot July day in 1947, in the Sheepshead Bay section of Brooklyn. He grew up in an apartment overlooking the Belt Parkway with his brother, Kenny, and his mom and dad, Rose and Morty. On every side there were aunts and cousins "fighting, screaming, yelling." Despite this, David describes his childhood as a happy one. He played a lot of basketball, watched *Sergeant Bilko* with his brother, and, aside from being a Yankees fan in Brooklyn, did nothing to stand out in any way.

LARRY DAVID'S SCHOOL DAYS

WHEN DID YOU FIRST START TO FEEL FUNNY?
Not until I went to college, when my feelings of inferiority and inadequacy really began to kick in. I was doing some impressions—Howard Cosell, Rod Steiger—but I never thought that I was funny. I blended into the crowd.

YOUR FRIENDS DIDN'T EVEN FIND YOU FUNNY?
The friends that I had in high school did not find me remotely amusing.

WERE YOU TRYING TO BE FUNNY?
No. In my circle, if you said something that you thought was funny and it didn't go over well, you were roundly criticized for it, and it made you feel like an idiot.

WHAT MADE YOU LAUGH?
I loved *Sergeant Bilko*. It was easily my favorite TV show. Bilko was this great con man who did things you weren't supposed to and got away with it. The humor was based more on character and story than joke driven. Probably the first time I watched somebody doing despicable things and loved him for it. When *TV Guide* did its list of the 100 best TV shows of all time, they named *Seinfeld* number one, and *Bilko* wasn't even on the list.

WERE YOU IN PUBLIC SCHOOL?
I didn't know private school existed. I had never heard of a private school.

DID YOU LIKE SCHOOL?
No. Like most comedians, I'm basically lazy, and I've always gone to great extremes to take the easy way out.

WERE YOU A GOOD STUDENT?
I was an average student—maybe a little above average. I remember my mother coming home from a parent-teacher conference when I was in sixth grade and the teacher told her, "Your son is very, very average." I couldn't stand going to school, never mind having to go home, get on my bike, and go to Hebrew school for another hour and a half. It was sheer, unadulterated torture. I eventually got expelled.

WHAT FOR?
One day I walked into the Hebrew school and I was late, and the teacher said, "Don't sit down. Where are your two friends?" I said, "They'll be here." So my friends Jerry and Sheldon show up

Opposite: Larry at 4, 15, and 30 years old.

and he takes us down to the rabbi's office and the rabbi starts yelling at me and I burst out laughing, which is exactly what I do on the show whenever someone yells at me. It was about six months before my bar mitzvah.

SO NO BAR MITZVAH?
My parents were beside themselves. They went to the school to talk to the rabbi. I don't know what they said to him, but they let me back in. By the way, I broke up at the bar mitzvah, too. Uncontrollably. There was one part I couldn't get through. You would get bar mitzvah'd with another kid, and every time I came to this particular portion, which was a Hebrew word that sounded like "fart," it would make my friend laugh. And so of course, when I got to that part, I heard him, and I lost it.

WHERE'D YOU GO TO COLLEGE?
University of Maryland. History major. I thought it would be the easiest way to get through it. I have a facility for remembering dates and phone numbers. But it was there that a self-deprecating wit began to emerge. I think it was because I was with people who had never met me before and it's possible, being from out of town, I was something of a novelty. It also had something to do with the fact that I had started to date and I wasn't very good or successful at it, so I could regale my friends for hours about my experiences. That's when I first started to feel funny.

SO YOU STARTED TO DEVELOP YOUR OWN VOICE?
Yes. You know, all I needed was one person to start laughing and I was off. I had one friend in particular. We became roommates and we just kind of took a liking to each other and he found me quite amusing.

DID YOU START TO THINK COMEDY COULD BE A CAREER?
I had no idea about the future. I didn't give it a thought. I didn't know what I was going to do. I was having a lot of fun in college and thinking, It's not going to end. And then all of a sudden it was upon me. Also, being funny around my friends was a far cry from doing it on stage for strangers. I don't think doing that ever occurred to me.

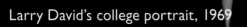
Larry David's college portrait, 1969

season one

HBO COMEDY SPECIAL: CURB YOUR ENTHUSIASM

ORIGINAL AIR DATE: OCTOBER 15, 1999 **DIRECTOR:** ROBERT B. WEIDE

Surrounded by a mix of real and fictional friends, *Seinfeld* co-creator Larry David is hired by HBO to film a documentary special about his return to standup.

> "You know who wears sunglasses inside? Blind people and assholes."
>
> LARRY DAVID TO OTHER COMICS AT LUNCH

INTERVIEWS

Jason Alexander
Larry Charles
Carol Leifer
Richard Lewis
Rick Newman
Glenn Padnick
Jerry Seinfeld

FEATURING

Linda Bates	*HBO production team*
Mark Beltzman	*mourner*
Julie Claire	*HBO production team*
Donna Cooper	*HBO receptionist*
Cynthia Coponera	*wife's friend*
Ed Crasnick	*Larry's suite mate*
Larry David	*himself*
Jeff Garlin	*Jeff Greene*
Eric Scott Gould	*Jeff Yerkes*
Allan Havey	*himself*
Cheryl Hines	*Cheryl David*
Michael Patrick King	*HBO publicist*
Don Lake	*HBO director*
Losmir Marin	*hotel clerk*
Susan Marque	*HBO assistant*
Suzy Nakamura	*HBO production designer*
Mike Reynolds	*himself*
Caroline Rhea	*herself*
Stefanie Singer	*HBO receptionist*
Suzy Soro	*herself*
Larry Thigpen	*HBO production team*
Becky Thyre	*Jeff's New York girlfriend*
Judy Toll	*HBO executive*
Allan Wasserman	*HBO executive*

IN THIS EPISODE

- Jeff Yerkes, who asks Larry for a recommendation, is the name of David's former assistant on *Seinfeld*.
- Larry swears to Cheryl on the lives of his kids that he didn't have an affair in New York, yet no children ever materialize for the Davids.
- When Larry tells the other comics at lunch that he started the whole "dick joke thing," he's referring to a bit he used to do in his act in the late '70s: "I hate my penis, my penis has no friends."

IN THE SPECIAL, LARRY TRIES AN OLD BIT FROM HIS STANDUP DAYS, AS WELL AS SOME NEW MATERIAL:

FROM THE OLD ACT

"It must have been very stressful to have grown up living next door to Jonas Salk's mother, I would imagine. You know you've got this woman, and you know every day the same thing: 'Estelle, did I happen to mention that my son Jonas, who your little Stevie never let play in the games or stuck him in right field, who never went out with the girls and wasn't athletic. Did I happen to mention that he discovered the cure for polio? My little Jonas! Polio! He's mine! I love him! My Jonas!'"

FROM THE NEW ACT

"Did Clinton actually think that he was going to get blow jobs from a Jew and get off scot-free? Obviously he was never with a Jew before. He thinks he's gonna get blow jobs? Blowjobs! From a Jewish woman! And that's gonna be the end of it? No consequences? What is he, crazy?"

EPISODE 1: THE PANTS TENT

ORIGINAL AIR DATE: OCTOBER 15, 2000 **DIRECTOR:** ROBERT B. S

Everyone's mad at Larry—Jeff's parents, who overhear him refer to Cheryl as "Hitler" on Jeff's speaker-phone; Richard Lewis's girlfriend, who thinks he's staring at her breasts; Cheryl, who figures out why Jeff left an apology on their answering machine; and Cheryl's friend Nancy, who is positive that Larry has a less-than-innocent bunch-up in his pants.

> "I get the distinct feeling that I'm like Himmler's ghost here."
>
> RICHARD LEWIS TO LARRY, AFTER LARRY SAYS HE DOESN'T WANT TO GO FOR COFFEE

STARRING

Larry David .... *himself*
Cheryl Hines ..... *Cheryl David*
Jeff Garlin............*Jeff Greene*

GUEST STARS

Kathy Griffin .... *herself*
Richard Lewis... *himself*
Sofia Milos .... *Richard's girlfriend*

FEATURING

Susie Essman .... *Susie Greene*
Mina Kolb .... *Jeff Greene's mother*
Antoinette Spolar Levine .... *Larry's receptionist*
Laurel Moglen...*hostess*
Louis Nye .... *Jeff Greene's father*
Robin Ruzan.. *Nancy*
Tucker Smallwood...............................*restaurant owner*

18

IN THIS EPISODE

- The show's theme song is "Frolic," by Luciano Michelini. Years before he had the idea for *Curb*, David heard the song on a bank commercial and tracked it down thinking it might one day be useful.
- David borrowed the name for the Dustin Hoffman movie he goes to with Cheryl's friend Nancy, *Hard Nut to Crack*, from a World War II poster that his friend, the late Marjorie Gross, gave him.
- When Louis Nye came up with his order in the dinner scene at Mama's Boy restaurant—"I'm gonna have the fish frenzy"—the other actors had to struggle not to break up laughing and ruin the take.

WHAT THEY WERE THINKING

Richard Lewis: "One of my favorite scenes ever was in this episode when I was screaming at Larry about Sofia. I was laughing when I said, 'Call me by sundown,' but I was really angry. It wasn't until I saw that scene later that I realized what the show was. Before that, I was overly concerned about how I would come off, but Larry said, 'Don't be concerned about anything.'"

Sofia Milos (Richard's girlfriend): "Richard must be the most neurotic guy I ever met. Just nonstop talking. Could you imagine being married to this guy?"

EPISODE 2: TED AND MARY

ORIGINAL AIR DATE: OCTOBER 22, 2000 DIRECTOR: DAVID STEINBERG

The Davids have a couples' crush on Ted Danson and Mary Steenburgen, who invite them to a Paul Simon concert after a night of bowling that ends with someone stealing Larry's shoes. Things continue downhill when Larry goes shopping with Mary and winds up insulting her mother, Ted, and a shoe salesman from Barneys.

> "Let me tell you something. Nothing, nothing gives me more pleasure than cracking an egg."
>
> LARRY DAVID, TRYING TO IMPRESS MARY STEENBURGEN AND HER MOTHER AT LUNCH

GUEST STARS

Ted Danson .... *himself*
Mary Steenburgen .... *herself*

FEATURING

Tim Bagley .... *shoe salesman*
Candy Ford .... *jacket saleswoman*
Anne Haney .... *Mary's mother*
Buck Kartalian .... *shoe repair guy*
Antoinette Spolar Levine .... *Larry's receptionist*
Joe Liss .... *shoe thief*
Lewis Mustillo .... *guy at counter*

WHAT THEY WERE THINKING

Tim Bagley (shoe salesman): "I remember in the breakdown it said they wanted a flamboyant, over-the-top gay type character and I told my agent I didn't want to play that. But she said, 'Why don't you go in and do what you want to do with the role.' Larry told me later that most actors played flamboyantly gay at the audition, but I came in real, not playing the obvious stereotype. It was a lesson to me that the breakdown might not always be definitive."

Mary Steenburgen: "After the amount of positive play we gave Barneys, I've always been amazed that they don't sort of genuflect to me and Larry when we come into the store."

Ted Danson: "One time we flew down to some place in Cabo at the last minute for New Year's Eve. There was this Mexican band singing old standards, "Blue Moon" and things like that, and Larry jumped up and started translating. He gave a line-by-line running translation of the song. It was so bizarre and quirky."

Mary Steenburgen: "I remember Larry showed us the *Curb* pilot in Martha's Vineyard, where we both have houses, because he wanted some friends' points of view. There were around six of us. I was just laughing my head off. Other people didn't know what to make of it, and I think one person even fell asleep. I think it took a little while for people to get used to the idea, but Ted and I have a similar sense of humor and we just thought it was hilarious."

EPISODE 3: PORNO GIL

ORIGINAL AIR DATE: OCTOBER 29, 2000 DIRECTOR: ROBERT B. WEIDE

Larry snubs a guy at his golf club because he doesn't like his bolo-string cowboy hat, and then later calls back the wrong friend by mistake and gets roped into an invitation to a party at a former porn actor's house. Jeff has to have bypass surgery and asks Larry to go collect his porn, just in case. Larry and Cheryl get lost on the way to the party (a small, intimate affair), where Larry breaks a lamp and gets kicked out for refusing to take off his shoes.

> "So what's the level of anger here? What am I dealing with?"
>
> LARRY TO CHERYL, AFTER THE PORN PARTY

GUEST STAR
Bob Odenkirk .... *Gil*

FEATURING
Sandy Brown ....*dinner guest*
Paul Greenberg ....*dinner guest*
Jackie Harris ....*dinner guest*
Melanie Hoopes ....*Gil's wife*
Mina Kolb ....*Jeff Greene's mother*
Nan Martin ....*woman on road*
Louis Nye ....*Jeff Greene's father*
Brian Palermo...*Brian*
Pete Steinfeld...*dinner guest*
Bianca (adult-film star) ....*herself*
Castle (adult-film star) ....*herself*

IN THIS EPISODE

- Bob Odenkirk's description (as Gil) of his bar during the tour of his house required many takes because it made David laugh every time: "That's a collection of small bottles and I like 'em… They're not as big as normal."
- Look carefully at the lamp Larry knocks down at the party and it's clear that it's being pulled off the table by a string.
- Shortly after this episode was shot (in which Larry can't work the Global Positioning System in his car), David taught himself to use his own car's GPS. "It's the only technological thing that I've ever learned how to operate. I really wanted to use it."
- Pete Steinfeld (who asks to try on Larry's watch during the dinner party) is David's trainer in real life, and also from Sheepshead Bay, Brooklyn.
- Cheryl tells Larry that he received a call from John DeBellis, the name of a good friend of David's in real life.
- Porno Gil's last name is Thelander, borrowed from the second camera operator on *Curb*, Patrik Thelander.

WHAT THEY WERE THINKING

Director Robert B. Weide: Weide pitched the porn storyline to David after the funeral of a friend. "My friend was single, so we sort of half-jokingly, half-drunkenly started to wonder if there was anything in his house he wouldn't want his family to find. That led to a joke between us that if one of us dies, you definitely go through the house."

Bob Odenkirk (Gil): "The show was fun to do, and I'm glad it went over as well as it did, but about the fake porn: fake fucking is a lot more like real fucking than you want it to be."

Larry David: "That line 'Pretty, pretty, pretty, pretty good' came from a bit I did on stage once that had to do with how you never tell your parents how you really feel. It was about my mother coming home and finding me with my head in the oven. She says, 'How are things going?' And I say, 'Things are good! Things are good! Pretty, pretty, pretty, pretty good.'"

Brian Palermo (Brian): "That was only the third episode, so they were still finding their way and would overshoot. They must have shot two hours–plus of seven people coming up with their worst porn stories ever."

EPISODE 4: THE BRACELET

ORIGINAL AIR DATE: NOVEMBER 5, 2000 **DIRECTOR:** ROBERT B. WEIDE

Cheryl stops talking to Larry after she returns home from a four-day trip and he pays more attention to the football game than he does to her. Larry decides to buy her a bracelet, but when he isn't dressed well enough to get into the store, he asks Richard Lewis to do it for him. Before they can get the job done, however, they help a blind man move into his apartment, and by the time they get to the store it's closed. Then Richard decides he wants to buy the same bracelet, and the race is on.

> "Are you questioning my sense of space, Larry? . . . Bring in the goddamn TV and be done with it!"
>
> THE BLIND MAN, GETTING FRUSTRATED WITH LARRY'S HELP

GUEST STAR
Richard Lewis.. *himself*

FEATURING
Perry Anzilotti..................................*restaurant captain*
Clement E. Blake .... *homeless man*
Laura Fairchild................................*restaurant manager*
Patrick Kerr ....*blind man*
Antoinette Spolar Levine .... *Larry's receptionist*
Robert B. Weide..............................*man with cell phone*

24

IN THIS EPISODE

- The restaurant manager (who gives Larry back his credit card) is played by David's assistant, Laura Fairchild.
- David sprained his finger and broke his glasses during his fight with Richard in the jewelry store vestibule.
- The interior office scenes were shot at David's Santa Monica office.
- David started to like the scruff he grew for the first scene so much that he bought a special shaver to maintain the stubble look.
- The attention Larry pays to his oral hygiene on the show mirrors David's life, in which he flosses his teeth a minimum of three times a day.
- Director Robert Weide has a cameo as the man Larry asks to call Richard's house.
- The lunch scene, in which Larry complains to Richard Lewis about having to tip a captain in addition to a waiter, was based on a lunch David had with comic writer and friend Bill Scheft in New York. As Scheft remembers: "We were at Shun Lee and he gets the bill and says, 'What's this captain's tip?' And I said, 'It's the captain, he got us the table.' And he says, 'But there's no one in the restaurant, we could have found this table ourselves.' And I kept saying, 'He's the captain, he's the captain,' and he started laughing. Before we got the check I said, 'What about dessert?' And he says, 'No dessert. I have a bet with Ted Danson: no dessert for a year.' So I figure Larry David, Ted Danson—this has gotta be like a million-dollar bet. So I asked what was the bet, and he said two hundred dollars. I said, 'Two hundred dollars? Have a piece of fucking cake.'"

WHAT THEY WERE THINKING

Richard Lewis: "I get so much satisfaction from setting Larry up and annoying him. I knew when we were talking on the street that if I told this blind man I had a fear of intimacy it would aggravate Larry and he'd start yelling at me. I prefer to give the assist when I know there's a chance for the audience to really see what Larry was like as a standup."

Patrick Kerr (blind man): "I'd never really done that improv-y thing, so I had no idea what I was going to say. But when we got to the apartment there was a plastic potted plant, and I asked the set decorator if she knew what it was called. As soon as she said 'agapanthus' I sighed with relief because I knew I'd be fine. That my character knows the name of the plant indicates a fussiness—I needed that agapanthus to become a complete pain in the ass."

Richard Lewis: "I knew that if I was supposed to be moving, there was no way I was going to look fresh as a daisy, so just before 'action' I made sure that I was doused heavily with water. It turned out to be one of the funniest still shots ever."

EPISODE 5: INTERIOR DECORATOR

ORIGINAL AIR DATE: NOVEMBER 12, 2000 DIRECTOR: ANDY ACKERMAN

Larry regrets a random act of kindness after it sets in motion a series of battles—with his lawyer, who charges him for reading a script he didn't ask her to read; with his doctor, whose waiting-room rules Larry finds annoying; with the interior decorator, who refuses to give him Diane Keaton's number after his answering machine garbles it; with two parking valets, who are having trouble getting paid; and with Diane Keaton, who is mad at Larry for blowing her off twice.

> "Let me tell you something, my days of elevator etiquette are over."
>
> LARRY TO JEFF, EXPLAINING WHY HE'S
> LATE TO MEET DIANE KEATON

GUEST STAR (VOICE ONLY)
Diane Keaton... *herself*

FEATURING
Rose Abdoo .... *interior decorator*
Jack Gallagher... *doctor*
Karen Maruyama .... *female parking attendant*
Kris McGaha .... *Diane Keaton's assistant*
Oscar Nunez .... *male parking lot attendant*
Lisa Ann Walter .... *nurse*
Marissa Jaret Winokur .... *woman in elevator*
Nia Vardalos... *lawyer*

26

IN THIS EPISODE

- Director Andy Ackerman told Rose Abdoo, who plays the interior decorator, to lay a surprise kiss on Larry during their brawl.
- David had a lawyer who took it upon himself to read one of his scripts and then charge him for it. David paid him and never used him again.
- All of the patients sitting in the doctor's waiting room are members of the *Curb* crew.
- The scene in Larry's lawyer's office takes place in the conference room, because when they arrived on the day of the shoot, the office they were supposed to do the scene in was being painted.

WHAT THEY WERE THINKING

Rose Abdoo (interior decorator): "It's really hard to watch yourself come on to someone and have them want nothing to do with you. If you watch when we're wrestling, Larry's trying really hard to get me off him."

Marissa Jaret Winokur (woman in elevator): "I remember we were literally fighting with each other 100 percent. I was like, There's no way he is going to beat me to the door. We were full-out beating the shit out of each other. I remember being face-down in the carpet like, This is insane."

EPISODE 6: THE WIRE

ORIGINAL AIR DATE: NOVEMBER 19, 2000 DIRECTOR: LARRY CHARLES

The only way to get rid of an ugly wire in the Davids' backyard is by humoring an annoying lawyer neighbor, who will sign an agreement to bury the wire only if Larry introduces him to his hero, Julia Louis-Dreyfus. Jeff's Fresh Air Fund kid burns down a cabin at camp and Larry gets the neighbor, who turns out to be incompetent, to defend him in the camp's lawsuit.

> ## "I got out of the nice business."
>
> LARRY TO JEFF, AFTER JEFF SAYS HE'S
> SPONSORING A FRESH AIR FUND KID

GUEST STARS
Julia Louis-Dreyfus .... *herself*
Brad Hall .... *himself*

FEATURING
Courtney Cronin .... *Jeff Greene's assistant*
Susie Essman .... *Susie Greene*
Wayne Federman .... *Dean*
Lucy Webb .... *Phyllis*

IN THIS EPISODE

- The little brown book that Larry loses is the same book David carries in his pocket for writing down ideas.
- David had an ugly hanging wire obscuring the view from his own house, and he and his wife Laurie looked into burying it, but decided it was just too expensive: "I know it's hard to believe that I would draw the line somewhere, but it's the principle. I didn't see how losing the wire would appreciably improve my life."

WHAT THEY WERE THINKING

Wayne Federman (Dean): "I think the improv process is easier for comics than actors—you listen, you react, you don't have to memorize anything. People are used to that structured Hollywood dialogue, but it's not even close to how real people talk."

Julia Louis-Dreyfus: "I was playing myself, although, to be honest, I'm not as aggressive as I come off. I don't tend to be so confrontational in life, and neither does Larry."

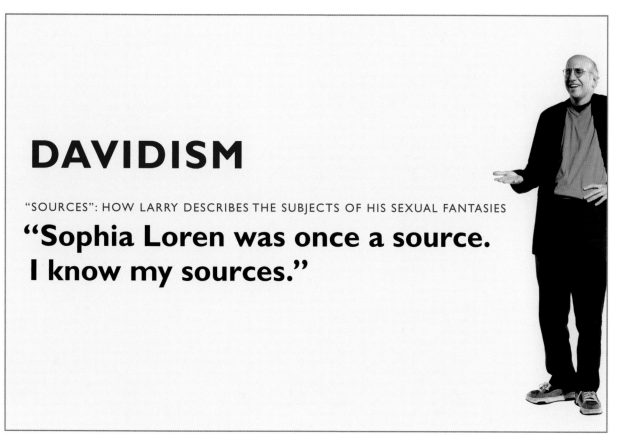

DAVIDISM

"SOURCES": HOW LARRY DESCRIBES THE SUBJECTS OF HIS SEXUAL FANTASIES

"Sophia Loren was once a source. I know my sources."

EPISODE 7: AAMCO

ORIGINAL AIR DATE: NOVEMBER 26, 2000 **DIRECTOR:** ROBERT B. WEIDE

Larry gets into a fender bender in Jeff's new '57 Chevy after he mistakes the beeping horn in an Aamco commercial on the radio for the horn of the car behind him. When a vintage-car mechanic at a dinner party Cheryl hosts agrees to fix it, Larry figures he's out of the woods, until a comment about not liking houseguests pushes him back in.

> "What is this compulsion to have people over to your house and serve them food?"
>
> LARRY TO CHERYL, ABOUT THE DINNER PARTY SHE'S PLANNING

FEATURING

Maggie Baird .... *woman in couple No. 1*
Clement E. Black .... *homeless man*
Pat Collins .... *man in couple No. 2*
Mike Hagerty .... *Aamco guy*
Allison Heartfinger .... *woman in couple No. 2*
Alexis Ross .... *caterer's assistant*
Kevin Ruf .... *man in couple No. 1*
Deborah Tucker .... *caterer*
Julie Welch .... *Julie*

IN THIS EPISODE

- The woman who plays Cheryl David's best friend is Julie Welch, Cheryl Hines's best friend in real life.
- The conversation about *Sour Grapes* between Julie and Larry was based on a real conversation between David and the husband of a friend: "I remember him not commenting, and I took the silence as a negative."
- Cheryl's hair was darkened for the first few shows because they had yet to establish whether or not she was Jewish. This is the first episode in which her non-Jewishness is addressed. Her hair color gets a little lighter each ensuing season.
- Larry asks Cheryl if they can go back to Colgate toothpaste, which David prefers in real life because orange juice tastes better after brushing with it.

WHAT THEY WERE THINKING

Julie Welch (Julie): "The whole idea when we were shooting the cocktail party conversation was to see just how boring we could be. We were talking about the difference between shrimp and prawns, and about moving from Covina to Downey, and how my husband's plastic-extrusion business was going."

DAVIDISM

LARRY TO CHERYL, ABOUT THE DINNER PARTY SHE'S PLANNING

"I'd like to make a little bet with you that I'm not close to having a good time. Do you wanna make a bet?"

EPISODE 8: BELOVED AUNT

ORIGINAL AIR DATE: DECEMBER 3, 2000 **DIRECTOR**: ROBERT B. WEIDE

It's a long, sleepless night for Larry when Cheryl kicks him out of the house for a typo in her aunt's obituary and for advising her sister's boyfriend to break up with her. Later on, Jeff also kicks him out for copping a feel off his mom, and the hotel where he's paid for a room won't let him past the lobby.

> "Hey, nobody likes to fly. I don't even like to drive. And I don't like walking. So occasionally I don't really know what mode of transportation to use."
>
> LARRY TO CHERYL'S DAD, AT CHERYL'S AUNT'S FUNERAL

FEATURING

Craig Anton	Cheryl's sister's boyfriend
Regan Burns	security guard
Scott Butler	man at gas station
Julie Claire	sunglasses saleswoman
Paul Dooley	Cheryl's father
Susie Essman	Susie Greene
Paul Goebel	gas station attendant
Karen Gordon	female hotel clerk
Mina Kolb	Jeff Greene's mom
Louis Nye	Jeff Greene's dad
Kaitlin Olson	Cheryl's sister Becky
Julie Payne	Cheryl's mother

IN THIS EPISODE

- Larry has a line about hurting his finger while adding a new hole to his belt, which David did for real that morning.
- If you look closely when Larry slaps Craig's (Cheryl's sister's boyfriend) arm at the funeral parlor, you can see that he's actually swatting away a fly.
- The woman who sells Larry the sunglasses is David's wife's niece, Julie Claire.
- Larry's advice to the other mourners is a quote from his friend, Tom Gammill, who was quoting Samuel Beckett: "Can't go on, must go on."
- Numerous takes of Larry shoving strawberries in his mouth were required before the cast and crew could finish the scene without laughing out loud.

WHAT THEY WERE THINKING

Kaitlin Olson (Cheryl's sister Becky): "There's something about Larry's face when you're yelling at him. He looks defiant and like maybe he's going to start laughing. It's so infuriating that it makes you want to keep yelling at him."

LARRY IN ACTION

Larry has lunch with Jeff.

JEFF	Hi!
LARRY	Sorry I'm late.
JEFF	Ah, it's understandable.
LARRY	Well I had to extricate myself from mourners.
JEFF	Why are you still wearing a tie? You don't have to wear it anymore.
LARRY	I don't know.
JEFF	If I didn't have to I wouldn't.
LARRY	Well I mean once you've got the outfit on you might as well just wear it 'til its completion. Maintain the outfit.
JEFF	'Til its completion?
LARRY	Yeah.

EPISODE 9: AFFIRMATIVE ACTION

ORIGINAL AIR DATE: DECEMBER 10, 2000 DIRECTOR: BRYAN GORDON

When an attempt to be affable translates into a bad, racist joke, Larry becomes uncharacteristically rattled. He forgets to pick up Cheryl's dermatitis medication, fumbles a bribe at a restaurant, and gets into a series of fights with Richard Lewis's girlfriend, a woman he didn't hire to work on *Sour Grapes*, and the pharmacist who holds the cure to Cheryl's skin rash.

> "I say stupid things to black people."
>
> LARRY TO RICHARD LEWIS, ABOUT HIS RACIST JOKE

GUEST STARS

Ted Harbert .... *Ted*
Richard Lewis... *himself*
Sofia Milos....................................*Richard's girlfriend*

FEATURING

Karen Bankhead .... *line producer*
Kevin Brewerton .... *party guest*
Robert Cesario... *maitre d'*
Robert E. Collier....................................... *party guest*
Donna Cooper ....*Dr. Grambs's wife*
Gregg Daniel....................................... *Dr. Grambs*
Gina Jackson .... *party guest*
Monica McKinley .... *party guest*
William Mesnik... *pharmacist*
Tyrone Alonzo Rouege .... *party guest*
Rachel Smith .... *party guest*
Kenneth W. Watts .... *party guest*

IN THIS EPISODE

- Although Larry botches two attempted briberies in this episode (with the maitre d' and the pharmacist), back in the day David frequently bribed ushers at Madison Square Garden and Yankee Stadium for better seats: "I haven't done this in a really long time, but you used to be able to get a much better seat if you bought a general admission ticket for a dollar fifty, and then for another five bucks you could get a box seat."

- Larry refuses to wait in line for a table at a restaurant in this episode, which reflects David's philosophy on waiting to eat in life as well: "It makes you realize the importance you're placing on what you're waiting for. And in the case of a restaurant, you sort of feel like an idiot. I think the last time I waited in line for more than ten minutes at a restaurant was the inspiration for the Chinese restaurant episode of *Seinfeld*."

WHAT THEY WERE THINKING

Bryan Gordon (director): "The first year, people would watch the show with their hands over their eyes. They couldn't believe he was doing this. They expected *Seinfeld*. I always said that *Curb* is an acquired taste; it's like lox, you have to eat it a few times before you like it."

EPISODE 10: THE GROUP

ORIGINAL AIR DATE: DECEMBER 17, 2000 **DIRECTOR:** ROBERT B. WEIDE

Larry accompanies an ex-girlfriend to an incest-survivors group that happens to include the director of a production of *The Vagina Monologues* that Cheryl is auditioning for. During the session, Larry makes up a story about an abusive uncle from Great Neck, Long Island, who, it turns out, just happens to be visiting L.A. on Cheryl's opening night.

> ## "Hey, I'm pro-vagina."
>
> JEFF, DURING A MEETING WITH LARRY AND CHERYL ABOUT *THE VAGINA MONOLOGUES*

GUEST STAR
Laraine Newman ....*Wendy*

FEATURING
Allan Arbus.. *Uncle Nathan*
Robin Ruzan... *Nancy*
Melanie Smith...................................... *Lucy Montone*
Cynthia Szigeti .... *incest-group leader*
Jane Edith Wilson ....*incest survivor*

IN THIS EPISODE

- The actress who plays Larry's ex-girlfriend is Melanie Smith, who also appeared on three episodes of *Seinfeld*—"The Hamptons," "The Opposite," and "The Raincoats."
- At lunch, Larry tells Lucy he didn't go to the prom, which was true in David's real life as well. "I wasn't aware of the prom. I had no idea that it was even going on, not that I would have gone. It's not the kind of thing that would ever occur to me. You would think I would have heard about it in school, but I didn't."
- The scene where Larry and Cheryl run into Larry's ex-girlfriend was shot in the lobby of the *Curb* production offices in Santa Monica.

WHAT THEY WERE THINKING

Laraine Newman (Wendy): "People have tried to bring improv to TV time and again, and it's never worked until this show. *Curb* is the logical next step from a 'herald,' which is an improv game created by Viola Spolin at Second City. Larry just evolved the form, and I was just really happy to be a part of it."

Melanie Smith (Lucy Montone): "Everybody just gets along so beautifully. Larry draws people to him who have a particular bent on life, and if somebody filmed the stuff off the set and out of the scene, it would be a show in itself."

THE IMPROV PROCESS: SEASON ONE

Curb Your Enthusiasm is an entirely improvised show. Every season David writes ten outlines for ten shows that cover the season's arc. The following scene, in which Larry meets with his lawyer, grew out of the three-sentence outline below.

Scene 4B from "Interior Decorator" (Episode 5)
Larry has an appointment with his lawyer, played by Nia Vardalos.

THE OUTLINE

4B. INT. LAWYER'S OFFICE
After some chit-chat about the script, Larry mentions to his LAWYER that he was surprised she'd billed him to read it. She feels it's part of the job. The meeting does not end well.

WHAT WAS ON AIR

LARRY DAVID	What is this?
LAWYER	Hi.
LARRY DAVID	What are you doing? Is this your new office? How come you're not in your office?
LAWYER	No, my office is being painted.
LARRY DAVID	Well, where should I sit?
LAWYER	Anywhere you want.
LARRY DAVID	As far away from you as possible.
LAWYER	Oh, that's very nice. Thank you. Very nice.
LARRY DAVID	I'll sit by the door, in case you come after me or something, I can run out.
LAWYER	Yeah. Larry, I ran into Diane Keaton's agent.
LARRY DAVID	Yeah. Uh huh?
LAWYER	What is that? What, what are you doing?
LARRY DAVID	Well, because I took so long in your husband's office that day.
LAWYER	Yeah?
LARRY DAVID	He kept me waiting for forty-five minutes because of his ridiculous policy, waiting policy that he has, that I missed my appointment with Diane Keaton.
LAWYER	Well, she's angry. You missed the meeting and then I heard you didn't return her call.

LARRY DAVID	Don't worry. Jeff set up another meeting for later. I'm gonna straighten the whole thing out. I'm a master of supplication.
LAWYER	All right. Well, that's good. There's something else I had to mention to you and I can't remember what it is—
LARRY DAVID (overlap)	Oh, I have something to talk to you about.
LAWYER	Oh, okay.
LARRY DAVID	Actually, I got, I got a bill from you for, uh, fifteen hundred dollars.
LAWYER	Mmm hmm.
LARRY DAVID	And I thought I was all paid up and everything, 'cause—
LAWYER	Right, it's for reading your script.
LARRY DAVID (laughs)	That's a joke, right?
LAWYER	No. What did—you're not kidding?
LARRY DAVID	Are you kidding?
LAWYER	No, I am not kidding. I read your script. I billed you.
LARRY DAVID	Wait a second, you read my script?
LAWYER	Right, that's—
LARRY DAVID	And then you charge me for reading my script?
LAWYER	I'm sorry, but that's standard practice. I think I charged for fifteen hundred, that's three hours and, you know, it took me like four hours to go through—
LARRY DAVID (overlap)	Oh, really? Oh, I'm sorry for taking up your time.
LAWYER	And you know what? Quite frankly, I should have read it, because it needs work.
LARRY DAVID	You know what? I am not interested in your creative input about anything. That's number one.
LAWYER	Well I'm sorry to tell you this, but I also gave notes on it and I'm gonna bill you for that too.
LARRY DAVID	Really? Really?
LAWYER	Yes, I am.
LARRY DAVID	Okay, well, I'm gonna take those notes and I'm gonna shove them up my own ass.
LAWYER	You know, that sarcasm is not working for me at all.
LARRY DAVID	Really? I'll tell you what's not working for me. You. You're not working for me.
LAWYER	Oh, I'm being fired?
LARRY DAVID	And you know what else? You're gonna have a tough time collecting that fifteen hundred dollars. I suggest you talk to my new lawyer, okay? Try, try calling my new lawyer.

In 1970, a week after graduating with a degree in history from the University of Maryland, Larry David packed up and moved home to New York to start his life. He got an apartment in Manhattan and spent a miserable few months blowing through a series of crappy jobs, all the while wondering what he wanted to do for a living. Then, one day, he had an idea.

TAXICAB DRIVER'S LICENSE

TEMPORARY LICENSE

T. L. No. 5021

LAWRENCE G. DAVID

This license is issued on a temporary basis.

Effective SEP 17 71   Expiration SEP 27 71

LARRY DAVID: THE MAKING OF A COMIC

WHAT DID YOU DO AFTER YOU GRADUATED FROM COLLEGE?

I moved back to New York and got an apartment with two of my friends from Brooklyn. Then I went to an employment agency and, armed with my very useful B.A. in History, got sent on an interview. So I got dressed up, put on my businessman act, and got a job selling bras. I didn't sell the bras; I sold the material that's used in the manufacturing of the bras. Remember I did that show on *Seinfeld* where George was a bra salesman? That was the company that I worked for, E.D. Grandmont.

WHAT WAS THAT LIKE?

I didn't have the foggiest idea of what I was supposed to do. I was beyond incompetent. I do remember, however, having to walk around with a brown grocery bag filled with bras. I got fired within two months and then got a job as a private chauffeur for an old woman who was half-blind. She insisted I wear my uniform, but I couldn't bring myself to wear the hat or clean the car. She couldn't tell the difference, but one of her friends busted me when she caught me without the hat on. Then I decided to take an acting class. I needed something to say to women when they said, "What do you do?" Saying I was a private chauffeur wasn't really doing the trick. Anyway, I didn't really like the class that much, but one day I was up in front of everyone and I stopped doing the text, put it in my own words, and people started laughing. And I thought, Whoa, that's for me.

THE BEFORE/AFTER MOMENT?

Exactly.

WHAT'D YOU DO ABOUT IT?

I sought out a guy I knew from college who I had heard was doing standup. We had lunch and I asked him, "Where do you start? How do you do this?" He gave me the name of this club in the Village, Gerde's Folk City, where you could go up on stage. So I said, "All right, I'm going to try and do this" and sat down to write some material, which turned out to be pretty bad.

CAN YOU REMEMBER ANY OF IT?

I know I did Rod Steiger's voice, but I don't remember what the context was. It didn't go well, but as long as you can get up once, you can do it again. The second time was at a bowling alley in Brooklyn, Gil Hodges Bowling Alley. I changed the material and took the subway into the bowels of Brooklyn. It was a little lounge in the bowling alley. It was totally ridiculous.

Opposite: Larry David was a taxi driver for a brief period in 1971. **Above:** David at age 30.

DID YOU GET MORE LAUGHS?

No, unless you count the two friends I brought with me, but even they were pretty weak.

THE PINS WERE RACKING?

Totally. Billy Crystal also played the bowling alley, and he used to do a whole routine in the voice over the loudspeaker: "Vinny, lane four!"

BUT YOU WEREN'T DETERRED?

Well I had nothing to be deterred to. I was living in a walk-up on West 43rd Street and when I came home at night I had to step over people to get into the building. There was really nothing else I could do, so I had to make this work. I heard about this club on the East Side, Catch a Rising Star, and I thought, Maybe this will be better. So I wrote a new routine. I wasn't talking directly to the audience yet, that was still too frightening.

CAN YOU REMEMBER WHAT YOU WROTE?

I wrote a telethon, to raise money for people who are unemployed. I got on line on a Monday night, and the line was down First Avenue. It was quite a step up from the other two places. I walked in the room and saw the big crowd and that was freaky, but I managed to get up and do the routine, and I got a couple of laughs. Then the MC asked me if I had anything else and would I come back the following week? I said, "Yeah, I got other stuff." I had nothing. But that week I wrote another routine about a 14-year-old kid who gets caught masturbating by his mother and gets put on trial. I put my mother on the stand—"Is it true, Mrs. David, that you've never been to Israel? Answer the question, Mrs. David, have you ever been to Israel?" Then she breaks down, "No, no! I've never been there!" I still wasn't talking to the audience, but this time I got my first really big laughs, which was more intoxicating than anything I'd ever experienced. After that bit, they invited me to start performing at the club as a regular. That was it. That's how I got there. And the rest is, the rest is hell.

WHY?

I'd be going on at 2 a.m. in front of five people, sometimes fewer. Then, after I developed more material, I started going on at the Improv and Comic Strip. Eventually I built up enough time so I could get weekend slots.

RICHARD LEWIS SAID THE FIRST TIME YOU SPOKE TO HIM YOU SAID, "MR. LEWIS, CAN I HAVE A RIDE ACROSS TOWN?"

He swears I called him Mr. Lewis. I deny that I called him Mr. Lewis, but I did ask him for a ride across town.

Larry David and Richard Lewis in the 1970s.

DID YOU WANT TO BE PART OF HIS GANG?

He wasn't really in a gang. He can be a very elusive figure. But once I got involved with comedians I knew that these were the people for me. You can say anything you want in front of them. They are an un-offendable lot. I mean bad material offends us, but that's it. I feel very comfortable around comics. You would just hang out at the clubs every night. If you were on at nine you'd hang out 'til two o'clock in the morning. Some comedians did Catch, some did Improv, some the Comic Strip—a lot of us did all three.

WHO WERE THEY?

Richard Belzer, Bob Shaw, Jerry Seinfeld, Paul Reiser, Carol Leifer, Larry Miller, David Sayh, Gilbert Gottfried, Bruce Mahler, Bobby Kelton, Ed Bluestone, Elayne Boosler, Barry Diamond, Glenn Hirsch, Jon DeBellis. You'd go on late at one club, then go across town and try to get on at another. We even had a softball team in the Broadway Show League. There was a whole life to it.

WHAT YEAR WAS THIS?

My first New York sojourn was from '74 to '79. Then I went to L.A. to do *Fridays* and I stayed in L.A. for two years after it ended, until '84. Then I came back. And when I came back I had a car and a good winter coat. You gotta have a good winter coat.

WHY'D YOU COME BACK FROM L.A. AFTER TWO YEARS?

I was doing standup out there and didn't quite know who the audiences were.

WHY'D YOU START YELLING AT THE AUDIENCE?

It was based on a feeling that they hated me and weren't paying attention. If things weren't going well, I couldn't take it. I really had no constitution for it. So occasionally I would get upset and storm off. I was very temperamental. And by the way, it wasn't like I was the only act. There were a lot of comics at the bar waiting to go on, so I didn't see the point of torturing myself or the audience by staying up there.

WHAT WAS THE ESSENCE OF YOUR STAGE PERSONA?

Well, my friends seemed to like me and find me funny, so basically I was trying to be that same person. But of course my friends knew me, audiences didn't. Also, when you're first introduced, there's a lot of ass kissing to be done with the audience, which I had a problem with—"How you guys doing? You having fun?"

HOW DID YOU BREAK THEM DOWN?

First of all, the audiences in New York during the week were not the hippest crowds around. It was mainly tourists, and not the ideal crowd for someone like me to be in front of when I was trying to develop an act. When we were shooting the special for *Curb*, I did a couple of rooms here in L.A.

that weren't around when I was living here in the early '80s, and I did great. You know, I'd walk off stage and I'd say to Jeff Garlin, "Where were these people 15 years ago?" There were some rough, rough times in New York.

DID YOUR PARENTS WANT YOU TO GET A MORE PROFESSIONAL JOB?
Well not really professional. Their aspirations for me were not that lofty, but they did beg me to take the Civil Service Exam so I could become a mailman. That was their dream. You get good benefits. The word "benefits" was used in my house more than any other word.

WHAT DID YOU DO WHEN YOU GOT BACK TO NEW YORK?
I worked on *Saturday Night Live* for the '84–'85 season, and after that I was doing standup and writing screenplays. Little things would come up, little projects. I did a pilot for HBO in '87 with Gilbert Gottfried called "Norman's Corner."

WHAT WAS *SATURDAY NIGHT LIVE* LIKE WHEN YOU WERE THERE?
I found it to be quite an easy job, and I really liked the writing. I didn't know what the big deal was about in terms of the work load, because you only had to write one sketch a week and maybe a news piece. But they didn't put any of my material on, which started to get annoying after a while.

WHY DIDN'T THEY LIKE YOUR MATERIAL?
That's an excellent question. Obviously the people in charge didn't think it was right for the show.

WHY DID YOU QUIT IN THE MIDDLE OF THE SEASON?
I had gone about five or six weeks without getting a sketch on, even though my sketches did very well at the read-throughs. So finally I just got completely fed up. One night, about five minutes before the live show, I got up a full head of steam, walked over to Dick Ebersol, the producer, and said, "That's it, I'm done. This show stinks! I'm leaving. I quit." So I left, and on the walk home to 43rd and 10th I started to calculate how much this temper tantrum was going to cost me. When I got home, I went over to Kenny Kramer's, my friend and neighbor, to talk about it, and he had the idea to just go back and pretend it never happened.

SO WHAT HAPPENED THE FOLLOWING MONDAY?
I just showed up at the meeting and the other writers all looked at me like, What are you doing here? Ebersol never said a word. I don't know why he never did—maybe he thought all writers behaved this way. All of this, of course, was done on *Seinfeld*.

WHAT WERE YOU UP TO POST-*SNL* AND PRE-*SEINFELD*?
I did standup and wrote a script or two. In 1987 I did some work on a talk show Joy Behar had on Lifetime called *Off Off Broadway*. We would do these improvised cold openings where I played a network executive and I remember thinking what a great way that was to work.

Larry David performs at the Improv, 1975

"He had a few different opening lines. The one he used the most was, 'I'll tell you something about good-looking people, we're not well-liked.'" JOHN DEBELLIS, COMIC AND FRIEND

COMICS ON THE COMIC'S COMIC

Friends of Larry David share memories from before he was famous.

STEVE ADAMS is a writer who met David while working on the TV show *Fridays*.

CHRIS ALBRECHT used to run the Improv Comedy Club in New York; he currently runs HBO.

JOHN DEBELLIS is a standup and former writer for *The Tonight Show* and *Saturday Night Live*.

JON HAYMAN is a writer and former standup. He played Chef Randy in Season 3 on *Curb*, and used to write for *Seinfeld*.

BOBBY KELTON is a standup who has appeared on *The Tonight Show* more than 20 times.

BILL SCHEFT is a comic novelist and former monologue writer for *The Late Show with David Letterman*.

BOB SHAW is a writer and former standup. He also wrote for *Seinfeld*.

ALAN ZWEIBEL is a writer and former consulting producer on *Curb*.

ON STAGE

BOBBY KELTON: As you've probably heard, Larry was not a crowd favorite. The audience didn't quite get him, but the other comics thought he was hysterical. He was too cerebral, so he didn't get a lot of paying gigs. One time I had him open for me at Grandma Minnie's in Philadelphia, and we decided to go see Constitution Hall. So we get into this hallowed room with the Declaration of Independence and there's nobody else in the place and he goes, "I gotta go up there." He climbs over the ropes onto the stage behind the lectern and starts improvising: "My fellow American citizens!" He's bellowing this out and all of a sudden this guard comes in and goes nuts. "What the hell are you doing in here? You could be arrested for this!" Only Larry would have the nerve to climb over those ropes and up to that lectern where Benjamin Franklin sat. I was mortified. Nobody would do that.

JOHN DEBELLIS: One time we were walking down the street in New York eating lunch and some bum asked Larry for half of his tuna fish sandwich. He ends up getting in a fight with the guy. Larry would draw that kind of stuff. He had this weird intense look about him, so I guess they would pick on him.

STEVE ADAMS: Larry doesn't have long periods of enjoyment. He's never blissful. There's always a "Yeah, but." But all of his worst qualities kind of make him chuckle. He's not anguished by his own shortcomings. He kind of accepts them.

CHRIS ALBRECHT: That was a unique time. This first-person standup comedy was happening for the first time. There was a lot of experience-based stuff, and there was tremendous energy because there were so many opportunities. Freddie Prinze, Gabe Kaplan, and Jimmie Walker had all gotten shows, and the guys from Carson were combing the clubs looking for comics. The entertainment business was starting to wake up to the great cache of talent that was in there. I think it's a little more fast food now. I'm not sure that the business today would have the patience for Larry that it did before. Back then his peer group was so certain that his talent was special. It's not as if Larry went from standup to *Seinfeld*; he definitely had a workman-like experience. But the reason he would eventually make it was because people knew how talented he was. Not necessarily because they saw it. You put him on stage because, even if he was going to have a bad set, the potential was so great that it was worth the time invested. I think the people from *Fridays* knew that, and then he took the route as writer.

> "He has an editorial slant on life and the world that few other people have. And those few other people dare not say it for fear of, oh, going to hell."
>
> ALAN ZWEIBEL

JOHN DEBELLIS: He had a few different opening lines. The one he used the most was, "I'll tell you something about good-looking people, we're not well-liked."

JON HAYMAN: It was a much tighter community then, it wasn't all about getting a sitcom. You did it because you liked it. You were surrounded for the most part by guys like you, you know, wise guys. Catch a Rising Star was the glitzy club and the industry hangout, where you were more likely to get discovered. The Improv's rep was as a club with a more artistic bent, almost true to its name. There was a bigger variety of acts; it was more free-flowing. The Comic Strip was the bottom of the barrel, and, ironically, the one that survived. It also produced Jerry [Seinfeld]. It's almost like the other clubs were a farm system for Catch.

ALAN ZWEIBEL: Larry was always the comic's comic. He was always the guy that everybody piled into the back of the room to watch what he was doing. He was funniest when he started singing, ranting, and getting overemotional. It was this controlled kind of Tourette's. It was something to see. People either loved it or they just sat there with their mouths open, like, What the hell is this?

CHRIS ALBRECHT: I remember one time at the Improv we gave him his intro and he walks up on stage with a look like he's in so much pain. I really don't think someone being taken out to the guillotine could be in so much pain. And he looks out at the audience with this look of disgust and disdain, more for himself than them, and says, "Ah, forget it."

JOHN DEBELLIS: I remember every week Larry would have a new secret to comedy. One week he realized that if he didn't wear his glasses he couldn't see the audience, and he figured that if he couldn't see them, he couldn't get mad at them.

ALAN ZWEIBEL: Pound for pound he's the funniest guy I've ever met. He brings an unbridled, damaged id. He has an editorial slant on life and the world that few other people have. And those few other people dare not say it for fear of, oh, going to hell.

OFF STAGE

BILL SCHEFT: One time me, Larry, and two other comics were in the car on the way back from playing golf in Westchester. We come off the West Side Highway on 57th Street and it's a bottleneck. They've got a cop directing eight lanes of traffic, and Larry's first in line. And we're waiting and waiting, and it seems a little long. The cop is waving every other lane. Everything with Larry starts out innocently enough. He rolls down the window and gives the smile and says "hey" to the cop. The cop doesn't look at him. Larry goes, "Hey, how about a break?" And then the cop makes a huge mistake— he turns to Larry and smiles at him and keeps directing the other traffic through. So Larry decides that the cop is fucking with him and he yells, "I saw that! I fucking saw that!" And the cop keeps smiling

Front row, left to right: Marjorie Gross, John DeBellis, Eddie Rabin, John Lenihan.
Back row, left to right: Larry David, Rebecca Reynolds, Elayne Boosler, Bob Shaw, and Richard Belzer.

at him and waving the others on. We were sitting there for 10 minutes. He finally waves our lane and Larry rolls down the window and says, "I'm reporting you, fuckface! I'm reporting you!"

JON HAYMAN: When Larry used to live in Manhattan Plaza I used to go over there to watch Knicks games and Yankees games. The real Kramer lived right across the hall, and we'd be sitting there and Larry would often be in his own world. They would leave their doors open like it was a two-bedroom apartment and the real Kramer would come in in his bathrobe and open the fridge and ask about the score. Larry wouldn't look up, would tell him the score, and he'd leave.

BOBBY KELTON: He thought his TV was a distraction and he got rid of it. He also had a list of excuses next to his bed so he wouldn't ever have to do something he didn't want to do.

JOHN DEBELLIS: I was in the office of *Seinfeld* when they got the pickup for the first 13 shows. Jerry was there, and he had promised to give Larry 15 grand towards a car if the show got picked up. So Larry looks at me and says, "John, I'm going to get a Lexus. I'll never be able to afford one again." At that moment he thought he had reached the peak of his career and would never earn that kind of money again. The great thing about it was that he didn't care.

> "We all kind of know each other, but Larry never liked to criss-cross friends. He kept us all separate. He didn't like to mix."
>
> BOBBY KELTON

BOBBY KELTON: In '95, after *Seinfeld* had become a huge hit, Larry bought a Porsche. But he felt guilty because he didn't think he deserved it. He took it back a week later and lost $16,000.

BILL SCHEFT: Larry is a far cry from the guy who would cook me dinner in Manhattan Plaza and say, "Oh, I have dessert." Meaning he had two ice cream bars in the freezer. Then he'd open the freezer and if there was nothing in there, he'd go across the hall and start screaming at Kenny Kramer, "It's embarrassing! I have company!"

BOBBY KELTON: In 2001, the Yankees were in the World Series and Larry calls me up and goes, "What's the score?" He's talking in a low whisper and I say, "Where are you?" "I'm at a dinner. I'm sitting next to Gorbachev. Can you believe it? Two bald guys sitting next to each other."

BILL SCHEFT: I remember early on in *Seinfeld* he desperately wanted to come back to New York because I think that he felt a lot of the pressure. He doesn't know what's best for him. He wanted the thing to be done with. I don't think it was a fear of success; I don't think anybody's handled success better than he has. I just think that he probably on some level didn't think he was up to it. Or didn't think he was up to it at the level he wanted to be. Of course he was more than up to it.

JOHN DEBELLIS: I remember when I called him up to tell him my mother died and he said, "I'm sorry. Do I have to send flowers? Because I'll have to get the address and everything." I said, "No, of course not. I know you."

ALAN ZWEIBEL: I think he's so fucking damaged. I don't know if he wasn't hugged enough or what. He's not like one of those Romanian war children who were rarely hugged and are lying in the crib, but he's like the Jewish neurotic version of them. It isn't very Jewish. If anything we've been hugged too much. Larry's been very open with all of us that on his birthday he never had a birthday party growing up. So what are we talking about? To a kid growing up, "Happy birthday" is commensurate with a hug.

CURB YOUR ENTHUSIASM

CHRIS ALBRECHT: Larry gets nominated for the Golden Globe for the first time, and I hear from people he's not going to go, he's not comfortable at these things. And I think, That's really stupid. I call him up and I said, "Larry, look, I'm not going to force you to go. I understand you're uncomfortable, but it would be really good for the show if you went. I think you have a really good chance of winning, and if you do win, it would look bad for everyone if you're not there." He says, "I'm not comfortable." I say, "Larry, I'm asking you go." And he says, "Is it a personal favor?" And I say, "It's a business favor." And he says, "No, no, is it a personal favor?" I say, "Yes." So he says he'll go.

So he goes, and he wins, and when it's over he comes up to me and says, "I really want to thank you for getting me to go. I really enjoyed the experience." And I say, "Can I get my personal favor back?" And he says, "No! You can't get a personal favor back!"

ALAN ZWEIBEL: We shared offices in Santa Monica, so the first year of the show Larry would talk to me about the outlines and use me as a sounding board. We'd order in lunch and watch the news in the lounge area, and I would throw in my two cents. The second year of the show he made it official. I think me having an official role on the show placated his guilt. I had to keep my door unlocked so he could come in and flop on my couch.

STEVE ADAMS: I think if you really look closely, every time Larry's questioning something or having a problem with something on *Curb*, he's just trying to get to the bottom of things. Why is an injustice happening? There's no malice, he's not nasty. It's not that he doesn't want to go to a party because people are assholes at the party, but because he sees nothing in it for him. And a lot of people share his sentiment. He can be a phony at a party for about 10 minutes and then he wants to get his coat and go home. It's just no fun for him.

BOB SHAW: There's something in Larry's anger that people respond to. Something in, "I'm going to tell you exactly what it is, lady. I don't care who you are. You don't bring in a penny and your husband picks up all the checks." People want to say those things, but they don't want to ruin the relationship.

BILL SCHEFT: The miracle of *Curb* is that Larry makes it totally believable that he would be duking it out with somebody over five bucks worth of shrimp. It was always that way with him. It's all principle. All the confrontations mean nothing to him. If you're a people pleaser like me, you would never get into these situations. He just doesn't care, which is what makes him so funny.

STEVE ADAMS: Five years ago my money was running out and I had what I thought was a really good idea for a movie and asked Larry if he'd come around town and help me pitch the idea. For two weeks he dropped everything and pitched this thing around four or five times a day. On the 17th time the idea was bought, and it became a movie that turned out to be dreadful [*Envy*]. But if he dies before I do and I speak at his funeral, this would be the thing I would point to.

WOMEN

JOHN DEBELLIS: One day Larry calls me up—this is in L.A.—and he says, "John, I'm in love with the popcorn girl. What should I do? Should I write her a letter?" So he writes her a letter that says he loves her so much he's prepared to give up meat for her. So we go to the movie theater to deliver the letter and Larry asks this kid if he would give his letter to the popcorn girl. Then we leave and we're driving around the block and I can see the kids are reading his letter. So we go back in, and of course they're laughing at the ridiculousness of it. So we say, "Why are you reading the letter?" And the guy says, "The popcorn girl's my girlfriend."

BOBBY KELTON: One time he takes his girlfriend Anna out to dinner for her birthday, and he has a two-for-one coupon. So after they sit down he excuses himself and goes to talk to the waiter on the sly. He tells him, "I don't want my girlfriend to know about the free meal." So the end of the meal comes and the waiter walks up and says, "Here's your check. I stapled your coupon to the back." Anna stormed out and later broke up with him.

JON HAYMAN: We once made a bet about who would end up going without sex the longest—not by choice. We were both complaining about how we weren't having any sex, and he said, "You'll get laid before me," and we made an opposite bet. Then one night I called him up and I said, "I guess you won the bet, because I had sex last night." He said, "You're kidding me!" He had had sex, too, and as far as we can tell it was at the exact same time, and this was after a period of months. It was a perfect bet, because what are the odds that it would be an exact tie?

From left to right: Kaitlin Olson (who plays Cheryl's sister Becky), Cheryl Hines, Larry David, and producer Sandy Chanley at a *Curb* wrap party.

season two

EPISODE 1: THE CAR SALESMAN

ORIGINAL AIR DATE: SEPTEMBER 23, 2001 **DIRECTOR:** ROBERT B. WEIDE

The Davids buy a house from Jason Alexander's agent, who tries to convince Larry that he should do another TV show with Alexander. Before he develops a show concept, Larry satisfies a lifelong dream and gets a job selling cars at a Hollywood Toyota dealership. He's about to close his first sale when Richard Lewis stops by and, upset that Larry told Jeff he was "high maintenance," starts a fight that not only loses him the sale, but gets him fired.

> "Can you shoot the whales from the terrace? 'Cause I like to have blubber for breakfast."
>
> LARRY TO THE WOMAN
> WHO IS SELLING HER HOUSE

GUEST STARS

Jason Alexander.. *himself*
Richard Lewis... *himself*

FEATURING

Chip Chinery....................................*car customer No. 1*
Jeanne Chinn.................................. *Barbara Schneider*
Apheon Crockett .... *car customer No. 2*
Rick Hall... *Tom Clarke*
Dana Lee .... *car customer No. 4*
Cynthia Martells.............................. *car customer No. 7*
Matt North .... *Jay Schneider*
Steven Pierce.......................................*male customer*
Shirley Prestia................................. *car customer No. 3*
Harper Roisman .... *car customer No. 6*
Susan Segal .... *real estate agent*
Abby Wolf .... *car customer No. 5*
Jim Zulevic ....*worker*

STARRING

Larry David .... *himself*
Cheryl Hines ..... *Cheryl David*
Jeff Garlin............*Jeff Greene*

IN THIS EPISODE

- The Davids have to move because *Curb* lost the lease to the house they rented in Season One.
- The meeting between Larry and Jason takes place in Jason Alexander's real office on Ventura Boulevard.
- Originally, the entire TV show storyline was going to star Jason Alexander, but when his sitcom *Bob Patterson* got picked up by ABC, he dropped out to star in it and was replaced by Julia Louis-Dreyfus.
- Larry starts driving a Prius at the beginning of this season.
- For the car-selling montage, David told the actors to ask him anything they wanted so his reactions would be fresh.
- In the editing room, director Robert Weide had to beg David to keep the line, "You're fucking up my shit." David thought it sounded too crude.

WHAT THEY WERE THINKING

Director Robert Weide said the car salesman idea was hatched on the airplane on the way back from doing some promotion in New York for the first season of *Curb*: "Someone asked Larry what he would be doing if he hadn't become a writer, and he said, 'I think I could really sell someone a bill of goods.' He said he'd be great at selling cars, and then he probably took out his book and wrote it down."

Larry David always thought selling cars seemed like fun: "I always thought I would be great at it. I know how to manipulate people."

EPISODE 2: THOR

ORIGINAL AIR DATE: SEPTEMBER 30, 2001 **DIRECTOR:** ROBERT B. WEIDE

Larry and Jason Alexander decide to meet to discuss doing another show, but end up fighting about where the meeting should take place. Larry upsets Wanda with what he thinks is a friendly hello. Jeff is splitting up with Susie and tells Larry he's worried she's going to be indiscreet about their sex life, which prompts Larry to try to prove how unkinky he is. A pro wrestler terrorizes Larry for playing "Cowboys and Indians" with his kids, but Larry uses Jeff to get back at him.

> ## "I'd know that tush anywhere."
>
> LARRY YELLING TO WANDA FROM HIS CAR

GUEST STARS

Jason Alexander .... *himself*
Susie Essman .... *Susie Greene*
Wanda Sykes .... *Wanda*

FEATURING

Jennifer Caldwell .... *waitress*
Dort Clark .... *passerby*
Kyler Fisher .... *Thor kid No. 3*
Gita Isak .... *passerby*
Mina Kolb .... *Jeff Greene's mother*
Deron Michael McBee .... *Thor*
Louis Nye .... *Jeff Greene's father*
Kenneth Schmidt .... *Thor kid No. 1*
Kevin Schmidt .... *Thor kid No. 2*

IN THIS EPISODE

- David had never changed a tire before shooting the tire-changing montage. To look more convincing, he refused to let anyone tell him how it was done beforehand.

WHAT THEY WERE THINKING

Wanda Sykes (Wanda): "I don't know if all black people like the show, but there are quite a few. I think because the show addresses race. It does it from rich people's point of view, but that's close enough. At least somebody's talking about it."

LARRY IN ACTION

Jeff and Larry talk about sex.

LARRY	The craziest thing I've done? I've been on the bottom. You know, that's it.
JEFF	Not even with your wife? Nothing, like, you know—
LARRY	Well, look what's happening with your wife.
JEFF	So you protected yourself ahead of time.
LARRY	I don't tell my wife anything. I don't confide in my wife. I don't trust anybody. I just treat her like an acquaintance. You think I want her blabbing about me to people?
JEFF	No, no.
LARRY	If we got divorced tomorrow, she'd have nothing to say. Nothing she could say. Or maybe she could say that I hate a couple of people, but that's it.

EPISODE 3: TRICK OR TREAT

ORIGINAL AIR DATE: OCTOBER 7, 2001 **DIRECTOR:** LARRY CHARLES

In one evening, Larry infuriates a Jewish man by whistling Wagner, lies about not wanting to play golf to spare the feelings of a filmmaker friend who's in a wheelchair, inadvertently comes on to the filmmaker's wife, and then gets in a fight with him for claiming his grandfather invented the Cobb salad. At home, Larry starts dressing in golf clothes and is victimized after refusing to give candy to a pair of over-age trick-or-treaters.

> "May I have free candy? I'm 40 years old, I want free candy."
>
> LARRY TO CHERYL, COMPLAINING ABOUT OVER-AGE TRICK-OR-TREATERS

FEATURING

Danny Breen	*Donald*
Randy Brion	*conductor*
Diane Alan Craig	*musician*
Rachel Crane	*girl No. 2*
Matrio DeLeon	*musician*
Matt Funes	*musician*
Stephen Kearin	*waiter*
Paul Klintworth	*musician*
Zane Lasky	*anti-Wagnerite*
Antoinette Spolar Levine	*Larry's receptionist*
Loren Marsteller	*musician*
Reggie McFadden	*police officer No. 2*
Kimi Reichenberg	*girl No. 1*
Michelle Richards	*musician*
Steve Skrovan	*police officer No. 1*
Rudy Stein	*musician*
David Stone	*musician*
Christopher Thornton	*Cliff Cobb*
David Wailes	*musician*
Holly Wortell	*Shelley Cobb*

IN THIS EPISODE

- David finds golf shirts to be one of the only appropriate displays of his forearms. "I don't mind short sleeves on the golf course; I just don't like going to work in short sleeves. Something about wearing a sanctioned short-sleeve shirt just doesn't work for me."
- After the anti-Wagnerite calls Larry a self-hating Jew, he starts to whistle "Springtime for Hitler" from *The Producers*.
- As he does in this episode, David makes substitutions when he orders the Cobb salad in real life: "Lose the bacon, the eggs, and the ham if they have it. Add a cucumber. Blue cheese on the side."

WHAT THEY WERE THINKING

Christopher Thornton (Cliff Cobb): "You don't find many good parts being an actor in a wheelchair. They don't tend to let actors read for parts that aren't in a wheelchair, and the stuff that is written is usually small and condescending and lame. I remember Larry was aware of the possibility that some people might take offense, but he knew that it was so real and funny it didn't stop him from doing it."

LARRY IN ACTION

Larry talks to the cops about his vandalized house.

LARRY	I was giving out candy all night. But, I don't have to get them candy. They don't deserve candy, and I don't deserve this. "Bald asshole?" That's a hate crime. We're a sect, a group. You can't call us bald assholes. What if we were gay? Then it would be gay assholes? That's a hate crime.
Police Officer No. 2	But it says bald asshole. That's to say, really, bald is not racist.
LARRY	Okay, but we consider ourselves a group of people.
Police Officer No. 1	Sir, I'm bald, I'm not offended.
LARRY	Well, with all due respect, Officer Burt, you are not bald. You've chosen to shave your hair, a look you're cultivating to be fashionable. We don't really consider you part of the bald community, with all due respect.
Police Officer No. 2	Did they threaten you in any way? Did you see weapons of any kind?
LARRY	No, there was no threat, except for the trick threat.
Police Officer No. 2	What's the trick threat?
LARRY	The trick or treat. No treat? Trick. It's a threat. How far can you take these tricks?

EPISODE 4: THE SHRIMP INCIDENT

ORIGINAL AIR DATE: OCTOBER 14, 2001 DIRECTOR: DAVID STEINBERG

When their takeout orders get mixed up, Larry assumes an HBO executive stole some of his shrimp and mentions this during a pitch for his new show with Julia Louis-Dreyfus. Later, during a poker game to try and make things right again, things go from bad to worse when Larry calls an effeminate male HBO executive the c-word, and accidentally convinces a dentist and his wife that he beats Cheryl.

> Larry: "He insulted me. He implied that I was lying about my stepfather."
>
> Jeff: "You don't have a stepfather."
>
> Larry: "I know, but I didn't like the implication."
>
> LARRY, AFTER STORMING OUT OF A PITCH MEETING WITH HBO

GUEST STARS

Julia Louis-Dreyfus .... *herself*
Brad Hall .... *himself*

FEATURING

Jane Carr .... *Fran Metzgar*
Frances Collier .... *social worker*
JoJo D'Amore .... *JoJo*
Laura Fairchild .... *HBO assistant*
Emily Kuroda .... *restaurant employee*
Ming Lo .... *restaurant manager*
Thea Mann .... *Melissa Halbreich*
Andi Masterson .... *dentist's wife*
David Morehead .... *Mickey*
Sam Pancake .... *Michael Halbreich*
Judy Toll .... *HBO executive*
Allan Wasserman .... *HBO executive*

IN THIS EPISODE

- Louis-Dreyfus and David considered pitching her ficitonal sitcom idea for real, but ultimately decided against it.
- Allan Wasserman played Kramer's roommate on *Seinfeld.*
- Louis-Dreyfus has known David since 1984, when they both worked at *Saturday Night Live*: "I felt sort of a kindred spirit with him because he almost got into a fistfight with Dick Ebersol, and so did Brad [Hall, her then-boyfriend and now husband] the year before. I really liked him for his anger."
- Brad Hall organized the deck of cards so that they could repeat takes and everyone would get the same hand each time.

WHAT THEY WERE THINKING

Julia Louis-Dreyfus (herself): "At one point, when I was yelling at Larry at the elevator post-pitch, Larry got the giggles and couldn't kind of take it. He said it was strange having me playing myself, that the whole thing was kind of off-putting."

Allan Wasserman (HBO executive): "My favorite moment as an actor was when I told Larry to 'take your 475 million and go buy yourself a shrimp boat.' There had been an article in *The New York Times* that week listing how much everyone from *Seinfeld* was worth, and for real-life Larry this was a fucking nightmare. I think he loved that line because it helped him deal. I'm sure he has his own *meshugas* about having all that money, but he's so open. When you're in the heat of a good improv, you don't give a fuck."

Julia Louis-Dreyfus: "When we were doing the pitch of the series to HBO, I remember feeling very nervous, as if I was pitching a real show. It was set up like a real pitch, and Allan Wasserman was sort of tense the way these executives get tense. Then I got tense, and I remember thinking, God, I'm kind of sweating."

Sam Pancake (Michael Halbreich): "The force of the c-word during the card game was truly there. When Larry said it, it felt really creepy and bad, and you could feel the energy in the room withdraw and everyone ice up. It felt beyond real acting, it felt real. I could also tell that people felt genuinely bad for me."

EPISODE 5: THE THONG

ORIGINAL AIR DATE: OCTOBER 21, 2001 **DIRECTOR:** JEFF GARLIN

Larry and Richard Lewis decide they have to find a new therapist after Larry sees theirs wearing a thong at the beach. Rob Reiner asks Larry to participate in a celebrity auction to benefit victims of Groat's syndrome, but Larry finds the pressure to be entertaining so over-whelming that he winds up offending the highest bidder during lunch.

> "His boys are hanging out all over the place."
>
> LARRY, ON SEEING HIS THERAPIST
> IN A THONG

GUEST STARS

Richard Lewis .... *himself*
Rob Reiner .... *himself*

FEATURING

Tom McGowan .... *John Tyler*
John Pleshette .... *therapist*
Mike Reynolds .... *waiter*
Raina Scott ....*singer*
Rachel Snow... *Melanie Tyler*
Robert B. Weide.................................. *man backstage*

IN THIS EPISODE

- David didn't want to use the shot of the therapist bending over in his thong, but director Jeff Garlin argued with him to leave it in.
- David came up with the idea for Groat's syndrome after thinking of former Pittsburgh Pirate shortstop Dick Groat: "I thought Groat sounded like something that could be a disease, and I remember Dick Groat being very thin and bald."
- David based the scene in which Larry's shrink won't talk to him in the bathroom on reality: "I once ran into my therapist outside of his office and it was extremely awkward. I passed him walking back to my table in a restaurant and he could barely bring himself to nod. It was like I didn't exist."

WHAT THEY WERE THINKING

Richard Lewis: "I went to this therapist in New York in the '70s who first made you go to group therapy, which was just eight or 10 people who hated themselves, whining. So Larry was having problems with women and I said, 'You gotta come to this group.' So he comes to the therapy and it was one of those nights where everybody was having lots of difficulty and Larry said, 'I can't stand this. I can't listen to these people whining.' And then he bolted. But when you bolt out of group therapy there's a chance that people might chase you. So we all chased him down First Avenue and he hid in a phone booth. Ten neurotics were tapping on the phone booth and we were like, You need us! You need us! He wouldn't come out and he never went back."

Rob Reiner: "Castle Rock, the company that I was a founder of, produced *Seinfeld*, so I was involved with getting the show started. We used to get into fights at the beginning and Larry would get all crazy. I remember him saying, 'I don't want to tell stories, I want people to sit around and observe.' He wanted to do every show about waiting for a table at a Chinese restaurant. When I said he had to do stories, he'd say, 'What am I going to do, *I Love Lucy*?' And I'd say, 'No, it's going to be your sensibility.' As time went by, he realized the wisdom of creating plot, and now he's become the master of it."

Rachel Snow (Melanie Tyler): "I remember I had a skirt on and the stage was all wood and I had to leap off this bench and spaz out on Larry. I still have wood-burn scars on my knees, but I don't care."

EPISODE 6: THE ACUPUNCTURIST

ORIGINAL AIR DATE: OCTOBER 28, 2001 DIRECTOR: BRYAN GORDON

Larry offers to pay his acupuncturist $5,000 if he can cure his neck pain, and then runs into an old writing acquaintance who, coincidentally, needs to borrow $5,000 until his ailing dad dies and he can cash in his inheritance. Trying to be helpful, Larry convinces his friend's dad to change his will, but before he gets to it he dies of a heart attack at lunch with Cheryl. After a misunderstanding with the acupuncturist's receptionist, Larry winds up having to pay the $5,000 after all, despite his not being cured.

> ## "You've got shy/asshole confusion, my friend."
>
> LARRY TO CHERYL, AFTER SHE CALLS
> BARRY WEINER AN ASSHOLE

GUEST STAR

Ed Asner .... *Mr. Weiner*

FEATURING

Scott Adsit	*Joel Reynolds*
Aki Aleong	*restaurant manager*
Jackie Benoit	*funeral guest*
Doug Benson	*Doug*
Joey Daniels	*funeral guest*
Jay Evans	*delivery person*
Stuart Gold	*funeral guest*
Koji Kataoka	*waiter*
Jeremy Kramer	*Barry Weiner*
Saki Miata	*acupuncturist's wife*
Michael Reese	*funeral guest*
Ruth Rudnick	*Carol Weiner*
Keone Young	*acupuncturist*

IN THIS EPISODE

- Larry's estate lawyer is named Joel Reynolds, after a real-life lawyer for the Natural Resources Defense Council, where David's wife, Laurie, works.
- In real life, David's neck pain problems were once so bad that he couldn't look up. He went to see Dr. John Sarno, who told him he was holding tension in his muscles: "I went to two lectures, and on the way home in the cab my neck started to feel better. Once I found out that there was nothing actually wrong with me, I was so relieved that all the tension went away."

WHAT THEY WERE THINKING

Koji Kataoka (waiter): "Ed Asner was a good sport. I had to nail him in the face with a glass of water about ten times in a row, and he took it every time."

LARRY IN ACTION

Larry and Dr. Moriyama discuss the terms of their agreement.

LARRY	I love your confidence.
DR. MORIYAMA	Wait a minute now, if I cure you, how would I know if you are cured or not?
LARRY	What are you saying? You're saying that I wouldn't tell you just so I wouldn't have to pay? That's ridiculous. I'm a man of honor.
DR. MORIYAMA	It's a family tradition, honor.
LARRY	Well, it's not in my family, but I'm trying to break the mold.
DR. MORIYAMA	All right, done.
LARRY	I hope you win.

EPISODE 7: THE DOLL

ORIGINAL AIR DATE: NOVEMBER 4, 2001 **DIRECTOR:** ROBERT B. WEIDE

ABC wants to make Larry's show, and to prove he's part of the ABC family, he and Cheryl attend a party at network president Lane Michaelson's house. When he finds no lock on the guest bathroom door, Larry sneaks upstairs and runs into Michaelson's daughter, who asks him to cut her doll's hair. Everything's fine, until the girl figures out the hair isn't going to grow back, and Jeff has to come to the rescue.

> "This is like Liberty, the Beanie Baby. Out of production. O.O.P., okay? Not coming back."
>
> ANNE MICHAELSON TO LARRY, AFTER HE SAYS HE CAN REPLACE THE DOLL

GUEST STARS

Julia Louis-Dreyfus .... *herself*
Susie Essman .... *Susie Greene*
Rita Wilson....................................... *Anne Michaelson*

FEATURING

Jane Carr.. *Fran Metzgar*
Una Damon .... *ABC executive*
Merrin Dungey .... *Amy*
Zach Grenier .... *Lane Michaelson*
Ashly Holloway .... *Sammy Greene*
Jonas Lagunoff .... *locksmith*
Ator Tamras .... *waitress*
Bailey Thompson .... *Tara Michaelson*

68

IN THIS EPISODE

- The party scene at the ABC president's house was shot in the home of *Knight Rider* creator Glen Larson.
- The shelf in Sammy's room fell down unintentionally in the middle of the scene, but they kept the cameras rolling and ended up using that take.
- The locksmith is played by *Curb* key grip Jonas Lagunoff.
- Running gag: At least four times in the show Larry asks people if they're going to attend the screening of Part 2 of the miniseries.
- For the show's final scene (in the bathroom of the screening room), *Curb* art director Michael DiMeo built a fake wall with a window for Larry to escape through after Tara Michaelson tells her mother she felt something hard in his pants.

WHAT THEY WERE THINKING

Bailey Thompson (Tara Michaelson): "Shooting was really fun because there wasn't a script so you could just be wild with it and do whatever you want. And Rita Wilson was really nice to me."

Rita Wilson (Anne Michaelson): "Larry is a friend of mine and he called me up and said, 'I've written the outlines for the season and I think this is the best episode for a woman this season, so if you want to do it it's yours.' I was flattered and excited and I said, 'I'll do anything.'"

EPISODE 8: SHAQ

ORIGINAL AIR DATE: NOVEMBER 11, 2001 DIRECTOR: DEAN PARISOT

Everyone wants something from Larry—a recommendation, a page in a birthday book, a thoughtful "goodbye" whenever he leaves a room. But when he accidentally trips Shaquille O'Neal during a Lakers game, suddenly nobody wants anything to do with him, and he couldn't be happier.

> ## "I'll have some vanilla bullshit latte cappa thing ... you know, whatever you got. I don't care."
>
> LARRY, ORDERING AT STARBUCKS

GUEST STARS

Paul Dooley	*Cheryl's father*
Richard Lewis	*himself*
Shaquille O'Neal	*himself*

FEATURING

Joseph Brown	*coffee-counter person*
Dort Clark	*splashed man*
Evette Dabney	*worker*
Mark De Carlo	*Albert Mayo*
Shelley Desai	*janitor*
Barry Diamond	*mental patient*
Angelo Dimascio, Jr.	*man in white coat No. 1*
Jay Johnston	*Jeremy*
Dan Kisella	*Bob*
Antoinette Spolar Levine	*Larry's receptionist*
Bob Margitich	*man in white coat No. 2*
Joel McKinnon Miller	*Dr. Craig Wiggins*
Brett Paesel	*Jill*
Julie Payne	*Cheryl's mother*
Michael Raysses	*doctor*
Mike Reynolds	*angry Lakers fan*
Aisha Tyler	*Shaq's girlfriend*
Terry Urdang	*Jeremy's wife*
Carlos Williams	*man in car*

IN THIS EPISODE

- The man who gets splashed by the bus is *Curb* prop master Dort Clark.

WHAT THEY WERE THINKING

Sandy Chanley (producer): "We weren't allowed to shoot the scene where Larry was tripping Shaq until after the Lakers were done with the season, in case anything happened to him. And we also needed the Lakers to win the playoffs in six games, or we wouldn't be able to get our second shooting day in the Staples Center. I became completely obsessed with the Lakers. I started watching all the games, and got completely inside the idea that they would win. So then they won, but Shaq was in Vegas celebrating. We were really lucky because the only reason we got him to do that second scene was because he was flying back to do *The Tonight Show*. In fact he was on his way from the airport to the Staples Center while we were still trying to figure out who had the key to get his uniform out of his locker. It normally takes two weeks of paperwork for anybody to touch that stuff. What was crazy about it was that it all ended up working."

Richard Lewis on going to ballgames with Larry in the old days: "Whenever we went to a game, Larry would make us move about 20 times. He knew every section, every row. He was obsessed. Once he'd get a seat, he'd start spying for better ones. He was fearless about getting kicked out."

Larry David on going to ballgames with Richard now: "I went to a playoff game with Richard Lewis once. He usually sits right on the floor, in the first row, but this time they gave him a seat in the second row, and he was complaining bitterly the entire time. He did not enjoy the game at all."

71

ORIGINAL AIR DATE: NOVEMBER 18, 2001 **DIRECTOR:** KEITH TRUESDELL

Everything's annoying Larry: Cheryl wants to throw out his favorite jacket, Richard accuses him of stealing his outgoing answering machine message, he can't find the plane tickets to fly to Cheryl's sister's wedding, and the Jewish man marrying Cheryl's sister is converting.

> "This guy's converting? Why's he doing that? You guys come to our side. We don't go to your side. Jews don't convert."
>
> LARRY TO CHERYL, ABOUT HER SISTER'S FIANCÉ

GUEST STAR

Paul Dooley .... *Cheryl's father*
Richard Lewis .... *himself*

FEATURING

Mark Boone, Jr. .... *homeless person*
Kenneth Beck .... *passenger*
Ed Burke .... *man in car*
Christopher Darga .... *man in airport No. 1*
William Fairchild .... *minister*
David Feldman .... *angry Jew*
Wendy Kamenoff .... *ticket agent*
Hiram Kastner .... *Jewish man*
Kevin Kendrick .... *Gentile man*
Joy Kilpatrick .... *agent*
Antoinette Spolar Levine .... *Larry's receptionist*
Sharon Nakadate .... *passenger*
Kaitlin Olson .... *Cheryl's sister*
Rick Overton .... *angry Gentile*
Julie Payne .... *Cheryl's mother*
Linda Ruffer .... *Jewish woman*
Jimmie F. Skaggs .... *man in airport No. 2*
Mitchell Whitfield .... *Cheryl's sister's fiancé*

IN THIS EPISODE

- The stolen answering machine message storyline came from David's friend Bill Scheft: "I used to have an outgoing message on my answering machine: 'Hello, this is Bill Scheft. Your screened phone message is very important to me. Thank you.' Larry used to say to me, 'I love that message like I love few things.' So in like the second year of the show he called me up and asked could he possibly use it in a *Curb* episode. I said sure, because everything is grist, and also I was very flattered. So he was going to use my message in the show, but he never did because I think what happened was he didn't want to deal with me having anything over him. The point is that I said, 'Use the message, I would be very flattered,' and he figured out a way to not do it and yet make the same point. He worked my name in, though. When he comes into his office and the secretary says, 'Bill Scheft called. He says you can call him back anytime.' I always thought it was his way of saying thanks."

- Christopher Darga (man in airport No. 1) played the limo driver in the *Seinfeld* episode in which Elaine pretends to be deaf.

WHAT THEY WERE THINKING

Christopher Darga (man in airport No. 1): "I made up that 'fucking douchebag' line on the spot, and I remember Larry broke and I was like, Wow, I made Larry David laugh. They also let me use my real name, which I thought was cool." (The line: "What's the name right here? Is it your name? No, it's mine. Chris Darga. See, if this was yours it would say, 'fucking douchebag.'")

Richard Lewis: "It was a heat wave in L.A. and they scheduled me to come at rush hour to do the scene where I accuse Larry of stealing my message. The air conditioner in my car was out, it took me three hours to get to the set, and when I get there Larry's sitting in his air-conditioned office making calls. By the time I arrived, I had rashes. I was a mental case. I walked in and said to the makeup woman, 'Where is he? I want no makeup.' I was in this heavy suit. I walked in and Larry started laughing because he saw how angry I was, and I swear I was ready to walk. I was like Bette Davis Lewis. I said, 'If you're so hell bent and honest let's do it.' I did the scene in one take and I put in what I was feeling, which was, How dare you make me rush over here?"

Larry David: "I've noticed that it's predominantly the Jews that make others convert. It's more important to the Jews in terms of the conversion. It's also weird to take on Christian beliefs after so many years. All of a sudden it's, 'Hey, I believe that this woman gave birth to this baby without having sex.'"

EPISODE 10: THE MASSAGE

ORIGINAL AIR DATE: NOVEMBER 25, 2001 **DIRECTOR:** ROBERT B. WEIDE

Larry gets a massage that takes a dirty turn and becomes so convinced that Cheryl's psychic is going to tell on him that he winds up blowing the pitch for Julia's sitcom at CBS, the only network left to do the show. Later that night at a restaurant, Larry steals a fork so the limo driver can eat dinner and gets arrested by the restaurant owner who is mad at him for refusing to stop-and-chat earlier in the week.

> "My mother did throw me against a brick wall when I was an infant. I didn't get hurt at all. I've mentioned it to her a couple of times. She said I was a little prick."
>
> LARRY TO THE MASSEUSE

GUEST STARS

Mike Binder	*himself*
Julia Louis-Dreyfus	*herself*
Nora Dunn	*CBS executive*
Wanda Sykes	*Wanda*

FEATURING

Tom Booker	*limo driver*
Jane Carr	*Fran Metzgar*
Una Damon	*ABC executive*
Zach Grenier	*Lane Michaelson*
Amy Hill	*psychic*
Burton Katz	*Judge Katz*
Eric Londa	*golfer*
Michael Pace	*police officer*
Sam Pancake	*Michael Halbreich*
Steve Sheridan	*Rick Crane*
Judy Toll	*HBO executive*
J. Keith Van Stratten	*CBS executive*
Allan Wasserman	*HBO executive*
Kathleen York	*masseuse*

IN THIS EPISODE

- In the scene when the masseuse is finishing Larry off, he cries out, "Pots! Pots!" which is stop spelled backward.
- The week this episode was going to air, David found out that another HBO show, *Mind of the Married Man,* had a handjob-from-the-masseuse storyline planned to air the same night. Instead of trying to rewrite the show, David addressed the issue by having *Mind* star Mike Binder appear in a scene in which the dirty massage is discussed.
- David heard Judge Katz's radio show in the car one day and called him up to see if he would play the judge in this episode.

WHAT THEY WERE THINKING

Tom Booker (limo driver): "I remember calling Larry an asshole during the middle of a fight, and then being told that calling him an asshole never really works."

LARRY IN ACTION

Larry is sentenced to wear a sandwich board that says "I Steal Forks From Restaurants."

JUDGE KATZ	Mr. David, I need your help in this. Obviously a fine isn't going to do anything. It just won't mean anything to you. You have too much money. So what do you expect this court to do so that the public understands that I'm not according you any special treatment?
LARRY	I could work at the temple on Saturday mornings. Hand out taluses and yarmulkes.
JUDGE KATZ	And you think this is a fitting punishment? Isn't it a joy?
LARRY	Well, temple can be quite grueling as you well know.
JUDGE KATZ	I'm gonna give you a sentence that will guarantee that you will never, ever do this again.

THE IMPROV PROCESS: SEASON TWO

Scene 9 from "The Car Salesman" (Episode 1)
Larry's first day on the job selling cars.

THE OUTLINE

9. INT. SHOWROOM

Larry with different customers, doing whatever he has to do. When specific questions are asked, he tries to bullshit his way through them. To one customer he gives a sob story — it seems he needs the money to pay for his ailing sister's doctor's bills. To another customer he says, "Come on, buy it." But at the end of the day, no cigar.

WHAT WAS ON AIR

LARRY DAVID	Hi, I'm Larry.
ARCHIE	Hi, Larry. Archie.
LARRY DAVID	You know what? My wife's name is Veronica.
ARCHIE	So, this is the Camry I heard about?
LARRY DAVID	This is the big boy, the top of the line. This is really as good as it gets.
ARCHIE	Oh, really.
LARRY DAVID	You know, you hear Lexus, Lexus, Lexus. We don't hear Camry, Camry. But that's what you should be hearing.
ARCHIE	Well, tell me, what's the, what's in the engine here?
LARRY DAVID	What's in it? Big stuff. Big, charging, crazy pistons. Nutty pistons.
ARCHIE	Is it twin cam?
LARRY DAVID	Yeah. Twin cam.
ARCHIE	What other colors?
LARRY DAVID	This is a fucking work of art.
LARRY DAVID (to a female customer)	What's your name?
SHIRLEY	Shirley.
LARRY DAVID	Shirley.

SHIRLEY	Yeah.
LARRY DAVID	That's my mother's name.
SHIRLEY	Tilt wheel steering, which I really like. Does this car have that? Is it standard?
LARRY DAVID	You know, you don't have the need to tilt in this car. I've never had a tilting need. My wife calls it Peppy. Let's, let's, we are taking Peppy, because we have two cars she says, let's take Peppy.
SHIRLEY	What kind of gas mileage am I going to get?
LARRY DAVID	52.
SHIRLEY	52 in the city?
LARRY DAVID	Depending on the city of course. Duluth is a city. It's considered a city but it's not as big as Brooklyn or whatever.
SHIRLEY	Oh. Okay.

....

LARRY DAVID (to a male customer)	That's my brother's name.
MALE CUSTOMER	Oh, really?
LARRY DAVID	Yeah.
MALE CUSTOMER	What's the wheel base? My wife is concerned about the car being solid.
LARRY DAVID	It's a thick base, it's a thick wheel base.
MALE CUSTOMER	I heard that these, SUV's, that they, sometimes they roll over rather easily.
LARRY DAVID	Roll over. Are you kidding? Look at this thing. Look at this. Look at this.
MALE CUSTOMER (to himself)	Jesus Christ.

....

DANA (new customer)	Dana.
LARRY DAVID	Dana. That's my middle name. Larry Dana David.
DANA	I notice this is a GT, and the brochure says there's a model called the GTS. Now what's the difference between the GT and GTS?
LARRY DAVID	Okay. The GTS is guaranteed tremendous safety.
DANA	So without the S it's just guaranteed tremendous?

....

LARRY DAVID (to couple)	How you doing?
WOMAN	Fine.
LARRY DAVID	Can I help you folks?
APHEON	How you doing? I'm Apheon.
LARRY DAVID	Apheon.

APHEON	Yeah.
LARRY DAVID	That's my stepbrother's name, Apheon.

Larry reacts to an announcement over the loudspeaker.

LARRY DAVID (to the couple)	That might be for me. One second. No, okay.
APHEON'S WIFE	I want to find out more about the car. You know, I want to see what the features are so we can negotiate some.
APHEON (to wife)	Babe, now don't be acting like—
APHEON'S WIFE	Apheon, what—
APHEON	You going to put a whole bunch of stuff back here.
APHEON'S WIFE	I like this car.
APHEON	What you need a big car for?
APHEON'S WIFE	I don't need to talk myself, I like this car.
LARRY DAVID (to couple)	Okay, could you excuse us for one second?(Larry takes Apheon aside) What the hell are you doing over here? You're fucking up my shit, man.
APHEON	Listen, why you pushing so hard to get this—
LARRY DAVID	Because she likes the car, she wants to be happy in the car.
APHEON	Maybe she won't be able to afford the car if she takes it off the lot.
	....
DANA	Is there somebody else who could help me with this car?
	....
ARCHIE	Look sir, I'm sorry. Thank you.
	....
SHIRLEY	I'm really not interested in buying today. Okay?
LARRY DAVID (to Shirley)	What? What, what are you doing? Shirley?
	....
LARRY DAVID (to young female customer)	Ever seen the Seinfeld show?
YOUNG FEMALE CUSTOMER	Yeah.
LARRY DAVID (to young female customer)	I'm the co-creator of the show.(She reacts) No, it's true.
	....
LARRY DAVID (to male customer)	Please, buy one, please.
MALE CUSTOMER	You'll sell a lot of them. You're a good salesman.

"For the role of Cheryl David, I had to imagine how someone could live with someone like Larry day in and day out. I think the only way Cheryl could have a good life is not to be bothered by most of it." CHERYL HINES

CHERYL HINES

When Marla Garlin, *Curb*'s original casting director, began searching for an actress to play Larry's wife, she wasn't precisely certain what she was looking for. "Larry never told me what he wanted," says Garlin. "I wasn't sure if he wanted someone like his wife, Laurie, who's very opinionated and smart and savvy, or someone who was the opposite of her." All David told Garlin was that he wanted the actress to be anonymous so that she'd seem more real, and that he didn't want to audition a million people. "I thought it would be funny to have someone who could push him around, someone Jewish, and someone outspoken, like Susie," says Garlin. "So I brought in a bunch of women who fit that bill, but he asked to see more. Finally, of course, he went for the opposite of what I thought—the shiksa goddess."

The shiksa goddess was Cheryl Hines, an actress from Florida who was then a member of the Groundlings Sunday Company, an improv comedy workshop in L.A. Hines's agent got her an audition at *Curb,* but an hour before her appointment, she got a call that her audition was "postponed." In fact, it was a polite way of cancelling the appointment altogether. Luckily, director Robert Weide saw Hines perform that same night, and was so impressed he made sure she was seen the next day.

Hines had heard *Curb* was looking for someone Jewish and a little older than she was, so she assumed she didn't have a shot at the part. At the audition, right before she and David began a scene about what they were going to have for dinner, he took her aside and told her that his character would be someone who doesn't eat chicken. Cheryl told him that was fine, and they started the improv:

Larry: "So, what's going on? What are we having for dinner?"

Cheryl: "Oh, let's see, we're gonna have some peas, and some corn, and potatoes, and chicken cacciatore."

David stopped the scene to ask Hines why she said they were going to have chicken for dinner after he just told her he wouldn't be eating it. Cheryl replied that he didn't have to eat chicken if he didn't want to, but that was no reason for his family not to eat it. David laughed, and realized he had found his TV wife.

It was Hines's ease with David that won her the part, and that translates into something believable on screen. "The other women who came in would either act too bitchy or too victimized," says Weide. "But Cheryl knew how to argue without it getting heavy. She was able to give back to Larry whatever he dished out without letting it get ugly."

Executive producer Jeff Garlin remembers how confident Hines seemed: "She came into the audition with the attitude of, I'm in control, this part is mine, and fuck ya'll."

ARE YOU LIKE YOUR CHARACTER?

At the beginning of the show I think the producers were hoping I would be Jewish and that Larry and I would be this Jewish couple. We were in the middle of shooting our first episode when Larry said, "I don't think anybody's going to believe you're Jewish." And I said, "I don't think so either." And he said, "Well, I guess you don't have to be."

WHAT'S YOUR RELATIONSHIP LIKE WITH DAVID?

I don't know why, because I've never really met anyone like Larry before, but he and I really just clicked as soon as I sat down with him. I can roll with a lot of punches. Nothing bothers me enough that I need to walk out of a room. I'm like one of the guys here. Larry can say anything to me and it would never hurt my feelings. I would never take anything personally, so I guess we're very similar in that way.

HOW'D YOU COME UP WITH YOUR CHARACTER?

For the role of Cheryl David I had to imagine how someone could live with someone like Larry day in and day out. I think the only way Cheryl can have a good life is not to be bothered by most of it. Otherwise she would be just as annoyed with him as everyone else in the world is and why would she stay? No one ever said they wanted me to be like Laurie David. I took my cues from Larry to let me know if I was on the right path or not.

IS IT INTIMIDATING TO WORK WITH DAVID?

I didn't feel intimidated by him. Before we started working together I had heard that he was neurotic, but when I met him he seemed perfectly normal. Larry and I have the same relationship off camera as we do on. I think he's charming and funny and I get him, but I also think he carries on about ridiculous things that I'm happy to point out to him.

IS HE NEUROTIC?

When I first started shooting, I was talking to Larry on the phone one day and he was in the editing room. He was telling me how the show was really coming together, and that I should come down and take a look at it. I told him I was going to take a shower and would come down in a little while. Then he said, "I don't know if I'm going to be here that long." So I told him I wouldn't shower. Then there was a long pause and he said, "I wish you wouldn't have told me that you're not going to shower. That's all I'm going to be able to think about. You're not going to shower? That's not going to work." So I said, "I'll shower, but I won't wash my hair." And he said, "All right, we'll see if we're still here when you get here."

CHERYL SEEMS TO HAVE THREE RESPONSES TO HER HUSBAND: CHARMED, ANGRY, OR A DRAWN OUT "OH-KAAAY."

For the most part I have the "okay" reaction. Which means: We all know what you're doing and what you're thinking, we don't need to hear this from you again, and I wish you would move on.

But why say all that? Saying "okay" is just a matter of being economical, otherwise I would just be arguing with him at every turn. I've read interviews with Laurie David where she says I'm much more patient than she is, but I don't live with him. I'm a lot lighter than Cheryl David. Cheryl David is very pragmatic. She's disturbed by a lot of Larry's behavior. For example, in the Porno Gil episode in the first season, Bob [Odenkirk] was telling all his porn stories and my character had to be offended and get up and leave. Whereas in real life, I would be the one telling my own tea-bagging stories.

WHAT'S YOUR RELATIONSHIP LIKE WITH DAVID'S REAL-LIFE WIFE, LAURIE?
I don't know her very well and had never met her before I started playing his wife, which is why everyone knows I'm not doing a version of her.

HOW DOES THE PUBLIC RESPOND TO YOU?
For a long time people really thought I was married to Larry. Some people still won't accept the idea that we're not married. People ask me how I could stay with Larry, or why I don't leave him. Or they say, "My husband's exactly the same way." A lot of times people will just hand me the phone if they're talking to their spouse and want me to talk to them. One time when I was in Toronto shooting, someone came up to me on the street and said, "Cheryl, how's your vagina?" In Canada, my vagina is huge.

DO YOU THINK YOU'RE LESS PHYSICALLY AFFECTIONATE THAN MOST TV COUPLES?
Larry doesn't think affection is funny. Kissing's not funny, and hugging's not funny, so why do it? Some of the directors and I have said to him, "You know, at some point you need to show that you guys have a good marriage. In most marriages people hug or kiss at a certain point." And he was like, "Yeah, yeah, we'll do it." He always feels slightly uncomfortable about it. Sometimes I have to be more aggressive in that department.

IS LIFE OFF-CAMERA EVER LIKE IT IS ON-CAMERA?
When we were shooting Season Five, Larry, Bob Weide, and I were in Larry's Prius driving up to the mountains for a shoot, and Larry put in this CD and turned it way up and it was the William Tell Overture. That's what he listens to in real life. He's the type of person that if someone asks him to have lunch and he doesn't want to go, he'll say, "No, I don't really want to have lunch with you. If you want to talk we can talk right now." And I'm like, "Why would you say that?" And he's like, "Why bother?"

WHO WAS THE MOST EXCITING GUEST STAR TO WORK WITH?
I found it exciting to be with Alanis Morissette. I just think she's such a great singer. Most of our guest stars are actors, so to have a singer on our show was a special day for *Curb Your Enthusiasm.*

HOW DO YOU LIKE THE IMPROV PROCESS?

Well, Larry used to not let me read the outlines ahead of time, and he used to tell everyone not to tell me anything, so before a scene I would have to ask him if there was anything he wanted to tell me. Sometimes he'd say, "Make sure to say that your parents are coming on Thursday and that they're going to stay for four days." But usually he'd say, "Let's just try one and see what happens." So we'd do a take and then he would give some kind of direction, like, "You shouldn't be so excited about your parents coming." Then we'd just do it again. He's very free. At the same time, this is why Larry has a bad reputation for dealing with people. When he gives notes, he's very direct and doesn't edit himself. One time a guest actress said something during her improv and Larry responded by saying, "Don't say that again, that's not funny. That's the opposite of funny." He says things like that to me all the time. Most directors might come over to you and gently say, "You're doing a great job, the scene's going really well, maybe the next take you should try this." Larry will just say, "Don't say that, that doesn't work." That's what I like about him.

CAN YOU THINK OF A SCENE THAT SHOWS HOW IMPROV CAN WORK BETTER THAN SCRIPTED DIALOGUE?

I remember shooting a scene in the Terrorist Attack episode [Season Three] that still makes me laugh to think about because Larry was so funny. Every time I'd ask him what he was going to do when he left town he would come up with something more ridiculous—he was going to go to a dude ranch or to Pebble Beach. Oh my God, we finally had to stop shooting because we were laughing so hard and just trying to collect ourselves. That scene wasn't even really in the outline, but just how serious we were supposed to be made it all the harder. Improv is really just about listening, so it's a very creative way to work. You never know where the scene is going to go or where it's going to take you. If something comes into your mind that you want to try you can just say it.

WHAT'S THE SET LIKE?

It's really a close-knit group. We all shared a trailer until last season. Shelley Berman has a joke: "What are all these people doing in my trailer?" I think the first season a lot of people would show up and be like, "Where's my trailer?" So the producers started warning agents that it was one big trailer. I remember when Ben Stiller and Christine Taylor shot with us. Poor Christine was breastfeeding, and she was pumping in the tiny little trailer with all of us sitting outside.

YOU HAD TO CHANGE CLOTHES IN FRONT OF EVERYONE?

There's a little bedroom in the back of the trailer, and we'd take turns changing one by one. It makes for a very interesting day. Larry is a different breed. When we started this show he asked me why we needed a wardrobe person. Why couldn't I just wear my own clothes for every episode? It was unnecessary to him to have trailers. We don't have a lot of down time on *Curb*, though. Most other shows that I have worked on you spend hours in your trailer.

Opposite: Cheryl Hines on set with Susie Essman.

84

DID YOU HAVE ANYTHING TO DO WITH YOUR WARDROBE GETTING NICER?

Wardrobe has been a bit of a challenge because it's a low-budget show, yet I'm supposed to look like I'm married to a multimillionaire. I think we've come a long way, there was a lot of Dress for Less the first season. Now I wear more Calvin Klein and this year even Chanel. If I hate something I'll say so and they won't make me wear it.

WHO DECIDES WHAT YOU WEAR TO BED?

Larry doesn't want anything sexy. He'll say, "You would never wear that." The first few seasons I was living in an apartment where the air-conditioning wasn't very good and I told Larry I would sometimes wear a strappy nightgown because it was hot, but that didn't make sense to him. He was like, "I don't think so."

WHAT'S YOUR FONDEST MEMORY OF THE SHOW?

It really struck me when we were shooting in New York and I walked into the trailer and Larry was sitting there with Jeff and Bob Weide and Larry Charles and Mel Brooks and Jerry Seinfeld. And David Schwimmer came in, and then Anne Bancroft came in and changed in the back of the trailer. And I just thought, This is so surreal.

AN INTERVIEW WITH LAURIE DAVID, LARRY DAVID'S REAL WIFE

In the mid-'90s, David's wife, Laurie, gave up her full-time TV producing career to devote herself to the issue of global warming, raising millions of dollars for the Natural Resources Defense Council. The couple joke that it is because of Larry's disdain for mankind that Laurie has been able to work on its behalf.

HOW ARE YOU LIKE LARRY'S SHOW WIFE?

Cheryl is his dream wife and I'm his real wife. She's a thousand times nicer to him than I am, so who can blame him for having a dream wife? The thing with the show that shocks me and that I cannot believe is how many people think it's his real life and that Cheryl is his wife.

WHAT'S THE MOST ROMANTIC THING LARRY HAS DONE FOR YOU?

Um, the guy doesn't have a romantic bone in his body, and that is the truth. He's much more romantic to his TV wife. I knew when I married him that I wasn't getting that.

SO HE'S NEVER SURPRISED YOU WITH A CHAMBER ORCHESTRA ON YOUR BIRTHDAY?

Let me put it this way: He hasn't bought me a present in 10 years. So I finally told him he didn't have to. He is the kind of guy who would go out on Christmas Eve to the mall looking for something. I let him off the hook on that one, and now I just buy presents for myself.

DO YOU WATCH THE SHOW?

I watch it with Larry when it's airing. I hate it when he and Cheryl kiss. It's just weird. I go "ew," and he just laughs. I don't like the show when it gets too dirty. I used to fight with him over that, but now he just doesn't let me know in advance what's going to happen. The day after the show in which "something" got caught in his throat, I was the lunch mom at my kids' school and everyone was coughing at me. To this day that still comes up.

DID YOU HAVE ANYTHING TO DO WITH THE CASTING PROCESS?

When he was casting the part of Cheryl I told him the only thing I cared about was that she be a brunette, that he didn't go blond. I think they dyed Cheryl's hair brown the first season, but she's gotten blonder every year, and now she's as blond as can be. But I don't care anymore. Don't forget, I was his wife during seven years of *Seinfeld* when everything that happened to us showed up on the show.

HOW DID YOU MEET?

The first time I ever met him I was a booker for the *Letterman* show and I went to check him out at a club downtown, the Duplex. I remember he was walking up the street and I went yelling after him so that I could introduce myself to him and tell him I liked his stuff. I told him I was trying to get him on the show.

DID YOU CONSIDER TAKING HIM ON WHEN YOU BECAME A MANAGER?

I seriously considered it, and then I realized he was completely unmanageable. He was a standup comedian who refuses to travel, which is like saying you're a pilot who refuses to fly. Although beloved by comedians, he was a bit of a nut case. He was completely uncompromising. He has never made one decision based on making money. He's only into the craft and the art. He's a brilliant standup comedian, as good as they get.

YOU HAD A DATE, BUT YOU WEREN'T INTERESTED?

I offered to be his friend and he liked that because he had this theory that if he had enough female friends that one would kick into gear. I remember having other boyfriends and Larry coming over and watching debates and sports stuff with us. I would talk about men with him.

SO WHEN DID YOU GET TOGETHER?

When he finally made a move he was chewing gum and it fell into my hair and he was trying to get it out of my hair and then he leaned over and kissed me. I think it was just meant to be. We were such good friends that it must have been underneath the surface all along.

WHY'D YOU ELOPE?

He wouldn't have a real wedding. He was against the ceremony because he didn't want to walk down an aisle. He also didn't think he'd be funny anymore if he was happy, but we got married in the early years of *Seinfeld*, so that proved to be wrong.

WAS IT HARD TO CONVINCE HIM TO GET MARRIED?

I had to break up with him four or so times before I could get him to do it. He was living at Oakwood Apartments in L.A., which are these temporary apartments for people in the industry. That's where he was living at the height of his *Seinfeld* success. We would break up, and he'd worm his way back in. We were engaged for three years.

SO HOW DID IT FINALLY HAPPEN?

I gave him a martini and said, "We're going to Vegas." He had a condition at the time, he literally had freezing cold feet. He couldn't figure out what was wrong and every time he'd see an ad for warm socks he'd order them. The day we got married it stopped.

"I remember coming on the set, and the only thing they told me was, 'Don't try to be funny.'" SAUL RUBINEK

MAKING *CURB YOUR ENTHUSIASM*

IMPROVISATION

In his seven years as executive producer and co-creator of *Seinfeld*, Larry David learned a lot of things about writers. The most important being that—with a good enough setup—you don't even need them. "When I was doing *Seinfeld*, sometimes I'd get to a scene and I'd go, 'Boy, this scene doesn't need me to write it,'" says David. "The situation is all there. You can just bring the actors in and they can do it."

With *Curb Your Enthusiasm*, David put what he learned on *Seinfeld* to the test. The show's improvised realism proves how writers' room sitcoms could become a thing of the past—although without David's talent for story and setup, it's hard to imagine when. A slew of copycat shows have tried to abandon scripted dialogue with varying degrees of success, but many make the mistake of equating improv with a lack of reality.

Of 50 *Curb* episodes, David says the few he isn't completely happy with are those without juicy enough ideas. "You start with one great idea and figure out what you can do from there," he says. "The hard part is story, because that's the engine of the show. You could get someone else to play my part, and it would still be a good show. There's no mystery to it. What's a mystery is the great idea."

"You don't get a sense of improvisation when you watch this show, you just get a sense of spontaneity," says Dustin Hoffman, who played one of Larry's heaven guides in the last episode of Season Five. "A lot of improv is repetitive, but this is a very legitimate way to make TV if you have people who know how to write on their feet like Larry does. A good writer like him can improvise so that it feels edited."

Or, as Gina Gershon, who played the Hasidic drycleaner in "The Survivor" (Season Four), puts it: "You throw out your clay, and Larry sculpts it."

ACTORS

Curb relies on more guest actors than a typical sitcom (an average of 10 per episode, versus 10 per season on *Friends*), the majority of whom remember *Curb* as their favorite acting gig ever. Patrick Kerr, who played the blind man in Seasons One and Four, says it's the one thing on his reel that he's really proud of; Caroline Aaron, who played Barbara in Season Three, hates going back to regular TV after she's done an episode of *Curb*; and Gina Gershon would kill to be a regular: "It's hands-down the most fun I've ever had on a set."

Curb is an actor's fantasy for

Opposite: Larry David behind the scenes. **Above:** Guest actors Patrick Kerr and Moon Unit Zappa on set.

many reasons, but the two biggies are that (1) no matter how un-funny actors feel while shooting, they can be sure that once the show is edited they will come across funny, and (2) the vibe on set isn't about fear. David's track record bought him creative freedom, and an unprecedented amount of confidence from HBO. When you create the most successful sitcom in the history of television, executives aren't as quick to tell you what to do.

Most actors who guest on *Curb* have the following experiences:
- At some point during an improv fight with Larry, they get up the nerve to call him an asshole.
- At some point they force Larry to break character, which gives them a sense of satisfaction. "I made him laugh once and it was one of the highlights of my life," says Laura Silverman, who played an overbearing saleswoman in "Club Soda and Salt" (Season Three).
- At some point, a day or two into the shoot, they discover that Larry breaks more than anyone else, and that he's a pretty easy laugh. "Someone calls me an asshole and I start cracking up," says David. "Take after take. They do it again, I laugh again. When that wrestler came up to that car window I died. Oh, it took a long time. And the scene where Phillip Baker Hall plays a doctor and chastises me for using his phone in the examination room—I thought I'd be there all day."

OUTLINES

Before production begins, Larry David writes ten outlines covering the story beats for every show that season. He writes in longhand on legal pads because he doesn't know how to use a computer— "What's the point?"—and then turns them over to his assistant, Laura Fairchild, to type up. Over five seasons, the show has gotten more complicated, and the outlines have doubled in length from four pages to eight (the Season Five finale was 14). On average, there are 15 scenes per show, each requiring about a paragraph of description. David might include some dialogue, but the point is more to set the mood of the scene than to tell an actor what to say. The following paragraph is taken from the outline for "Ted and Mary," the second episode of Season One.

......

3. INT. LARRY AND CHERYL'S KITCHEN—NEXT MORNING
Larry's alone reading the paper. Phone rings. It's Mary. They tell each other what a great time they had. Mary mentions that she's going shopping. Larry says, "Shopping? You know, I could use a few things. Where you going?" She tells him Barneys, and Larry makes plans to meet her there.

......

The outlines are kept classified to prevent plot leaks and—David's biggest fear—to discourage actors from preparing lines. "I remember coming on the set, and the only thing they told me was, 'Don't try to be funny,'" says Saul Rubinek (Dr. Leo Funkhouser, Season Four). It's so important to David to preserve the possibility of a completely fresh response that for the first two seasons he wouldn't even show the outlines to Cheryl Hines, his on-screen wife. "I really didn't know what was going on," says Hines. "I would come to the set and ask the hair-and-makeup people if they knew anything about the previous scenes, but they weren't allowed to tell me anything. Larry would say,

'I would show you, but I don't want you to come in here with lines that you think are going to be funny.'" Hines finally convinced David to let her read the outlines if she promised to completely forget about them afterward.

Hines kept her promise, but it wasn't as easy for every actor to ignore the instinct to prepare for a scene. For the first two seasons David wouldn't let Richard Lewis see the outline until the night before shooting, which he later changed to the morning of. "People in the show got it earlier, but they would keep the outline from me until the last second," says Lewis. "I was an annoyance to Larry—faxing and calling and bothering the shit out of him. He would hide from me. Christ, he was like a bullfighter."

AUDITION

Curb is 100 percent improvised, so for those who try out, the audition is a lot like a rehearsal. Bigger names (Rob Reiner, Rita Wilson) don't audition, but those who are less well-known are delighted to discover (even when not cast) that David will be improvising with them. Actors are told in advance what role they're auditioning for—Norwegian golf pro, sex offender, Barneys salesman—but don't get any context until they arrive at the Santa Monica production offices. Mayim Bialik, who played a former lesbian in Season Five, was handed a slip of paper with a premise that read: "You run into Larry and Jeff in a restaurant. You're excited to see Larry, but not Jeff. You ask them if they're coming to your parents' anniversary party." She was then given a few minutes to think before being invited into a casting room that included Larry David, Larry Charles (who directed the episode), executive producers Robert Weide and Jeff Garlin, and the casting director, Allison Jones. Chris Williams showed up for his audition for "Krazee-Eyez Killa" (Season Three) dressed like a rapper. The Georgetown grad was so worried he wouldn't be taken seriously as a hardcore rapper that he walked into a non-*Curb* office in the same building to test-drive his character in front of a receptionist. She wasn't the only one fooled. It wasn't until the end of the first day of shooting (when he was confident that he wasn't going to get fired) that he admitted his real identity.

ON SET

Curb is shot almost entirely on location over the course of six months, and edited over six more. David appears in almost every scene, but he spends a fair bit of time between takes whistling, doing the crossword, or practicing his golf swing. During Season Three, David and some guys in the crew became obsessed with the crossword puzzle in the *L.A. Times* and would try to finish it before Shelley Berman (who can complete it any day of the week in less than an hour) could get to it. During Season Five, to help David improve his golf swing, the crew built him a helmet that dinged whenever he even slightly moved his head.

EDITING

Because *Curb Your Enthusiasm* shoots so much more footage than they use, it is one of the hardest half-hours on television to edit. With an average ratio of 30 minutes shot to every one minute used, each show takes around four to five weeks to edit, closer to documentary film than TV.

The first step is up to the show's two editors, Steve Rasch and Jon Corn, who screen every frame of the episode and put together an initial cut. The first season was the most difficult to edit because there was a tighter lid on the budget, and only a couple of takes to choose from for each scene. By the second season, they started to shoot 30 minutes for every one used, and by the end of Season Five the ratio was up to 40 to one. "Once we got the rhythm of doing the show down, we could shoot twice as much footage, because we could handle editing it," says Rasch, who has been with *Curb* since the special. "It took us a season or two to find our way, and for Larry to become confident in what he wanted."

By the second season there was enough money always to have two cameras shooting, one of which was focused on Larry. "He drives the scenes, and his mind is ahead of everybody in the improv," says Rasch. "He says things off the top of his head that are brilliant, and then he never says them again. You have to have the camera on him all the time or you're going to lose it." Extra attention is paid to a scene's important comedy moment, like when Larry gagged on Mary Steenburgen's mother's water during lunch in Season One. These scenes are usually shot ten different ways to provide more choice in editing.

Before *Curb*, there weren't any shows on TV that used the slightly moving hand-held camera that makes viewers feel like voyeurs. One of the first things actors are told on sitcoms is never to let lines overlap, but David encourages overlapping dialogue on *Curb* because it's how people really talk, and it makes everything feel more real. A number of shows have since borrowed this trick.

For an editor, overlapping dialogue is a challenge. It's impossible to cut to the next line while someone is murmuring something indecipherable in the background. To get rid of the overlap, Rasch and Corn steal words from other takes, or have actors loop the lines that need to be repaired.

The editors on *Curb* are essentially taking an unscripted show and making it sound more scripted. "What I'm hired to do is make good sentences," says Rasch. "The grammar is very important. If it comes in the door and the talk isn't clean, the idea is to patch together good sentences."

They're not all they have to patch together. "The first season, Larry had a lot of discomfort with the smoochy stuff with Cheryl," says Rasch. "He really likes Cheryl and they can hug and touch no problem on the set, but when the camera rolls he turns into a 16-year-old actor, and we have to dance around it and make it look real." For the scene in the last show of Season Five in which he plants a passionate kiss on Cheryl, Rasch had to edit together two different takes to get a kiss that was long enough.

For each half-hour show, Rasch and Corn make between 300 and 400 picture edits. Underneath the picture, they have to make an additional 500 audio edits to massage the dialogue into something clear. How many of their original edits survive depends on the individual show. "By this point I know that they trust me and that the things that aren't right aren't my fault," says Corn. "My goal is to turn in something that's airable."

"Sometimes I'm in the groove and I can anticipate, and two-thirds to three-quarters of my work survives," says Rasch. "That's a good show. But I love sitting there and showing them my half-hour version and thinking, Hey, beat this."

IN SEARCH OF A NAME

"When titles are on your mind, anything you hear, any phrase, you think about as a potential title," says David. "I heard the expression and it jumped out and stayed with me." David thought "Curb Your Enthusiasm" said a lot in three words: "Maybe not everybody's as happy as you are and you shouldn't go around shoving it in everybody's faces. I actually find it more disconcerting than a public display of affection. There's something funny about it, too—happiness is upsetting. Other people's good fortune is upsetting."

Months before "Curb Your Enthusiasm" became the official title of the HBO special, director Bob Weide started keeping a list of potential titles as they occurred to him (below). Weide liked "Regrets Only," but David thought it sounded too much like a Richard Lewis special. Weide's opinion wouldn't have mattered anyway, because David had liked "Curb Your Enthusiasm" since the day he thought of it. In fact, when HBO picked up the show for series, president Carolyn Strauss begged David not to saddle the series with such a long, hard-to-remember name. But it was too late—he liked the ring of it.

LARRY DAVID PROJECT
POSSIBLE TITLES

Larry David...

Life Be Not Proud
Nowhere Fast
Nothing Ventured
Curb Your Enthusiasm
Kicking and Screaming
Going Backwards
Half Empty
Do Not Go Gently
Out of the Loop
With Friends Like These
Best Foot Backwards
Something So Wrong
Push Comes To Shove
Regrets Only
No Life To Live
The Shame Must Go On
Dead On The Inside

Larry David Vanity Project

Larry:
See if any of these strike your fancy. I'm going to lay a temp title on before Monday.
—Bob

"He's a very patient person when it comes to comedy. He's so confident of where he's going that he's willing to throw away laughs along the way because they will distract or diffuse or undermine the laughter he's really going for." LARRY CHARLES

DIRECTORS ON DIRECTING

When he first started thinking about the look and feel of the *Curb Your Enthusiasm* hour-long special, Larry David revisited some of the ideas he had originally proposed (and NBC had rejected) for *Seinfeld.* His main requirement was that the show feel more real than anything else on TV, so he devised a list of conditions that were ground-breaking in their simplicity: the show would be shot using a hand-held camera, in sequence, on location, and without a script.

When it came to directing an improvised show, David decided to hire people he trusted, and let them figure it out for themselves. To prepare for a shoot, all a *Curb* director really needs to do is read the episode outline and show up. On set, he walks the actors through basic blocking (with the actors substituting "blah blah" for real dialogue) and then starts to shoot.

Unlike on a traditional sitcom, the cameras on *Curb* never stop rolling. Directors and actors realize that a lot of pre-planning is pointless because they can shoot a scene a dozen different times and cherry pick their favorite take in editing. This works because David doesn't want actors to look like they're acting, and he doesn't want the show to look directed. For extremely complicated scenes, like the dodgeball game in "The Grand Opening" (Season Three), directors might draw a storyboard beforehand, but on an average day, they tend to direct as they go.

To capture the action, there are two cameramen who not only have to follow the actors around, but stay out of each other's shots. "They're like a jazz band the way they move around," says Caroline Aaron, who plays Barbara in "Chet's Shirt" (Season Three). "They have no idea where the actors are going to go, but they move like this well-oiled machine."

After each take, David, the director, and executive producers Jeff Garlin, Robert Weide, and Larry Charles usually huddle to discuss the performance. Guest actors never know what to expect, but as soon as they realize they can trust the director, they start having fun. "I love being on the set of this show," says Bob Einstein (who plays Marty Funkhouser). "It ends up being a really controlled version of insanity."

ROBERT WEIDE

To direct the original HBO special, David hired friend and documentary filmmaker Robert Weide. Weide created a template for directing *Curb,* and went on to direct more than half the episodes.

As a director, Weide is good at making actors comfortable, and often acts as a go-between: "If I have a feeling about an actor's performance I'll tell Larry, and if he agrees he'll say, 'You're right, tell him.'" For Weide, the secret to directing *Curb* is knowing when to inflict yourself on it, and when to stand back. In fact, he says that his job as director boils down to coming up

Director Robert Weide on set with Larry David.

with a game plan for a scene, and then selling David on the idea. "Sometimes I'll think of some stylistic flourish to add to the scene, but Larry usually figures it will be the first thing cut in the editing room." Generally David accepts his vision, but Weide says he isn't territorial. "My job is ultimately to give Larry what he wants," says Weide.

The protocol among *Curb* directors is to run ideas by David first, but sometimes Weide will sneak suggestions to actors in order to get a more natural response. The night before they shot the opening party scene in "Krazee-Eyez Killa," Weide asked Chris Williams to make up lyrics to a rap song to sing to Larry. This is helpful because David is generally the only actor in a scene who knows the overall arc of the show. "To me, it would have been unfair to make Chris come up with lyrics on the spot," says Weide.

Weide's goal is to walk the line between real and funny, but in the end, he thinks the trick of directing comes down to casting: "If you cast the right people there's not a lot to do except get your shots and stay out of the way."

LARRY CHARLES

Executive producer and director Larry Charles met Larry David working on *Fridays* in the '80s, and later wrote for *Seinfeld*. The Larrys grew up in neighboring sections of Brooklyn, which informed the shorthand that exists between them to this day. "We both grew up under the subway, which forces you to be loud and quick," says Charles. "If you wanted to get your words heard in between the Brighton Beach El, you had to talk fast, and you had to talk too loud."

Charles is a generation younger than David, but he describes their personalities as similarly volatile. "We care very passionately and intensely about the integrity of what we are doing," says Charles. "Even on *Fridays,* we were always both exploding in typical Brooklyn temperamental fashion. We also had many of the same reference points, so a lot of the same stuff made us laugh.'"

Charles says the Larry David you meet today is a slightly mellowed version of the one he met in the early '80s, but essentially the same man. "To try to pin him down as being about one specific thing really misses the point about Larry David's brilliance," says Charles. "He grew up in a certain era, and he's not just interested in *Sergeant Bilko,* but in history, and war, and Communism. All those things kind of contribute to his character, and standup, and storytelling, and personality."

As a director, Charles says his sensibility is darker than the other directors'. "Larry and I have developed a trust, so he allows me to push him into the darkest recesses of his psyche, and he's willing to go there because he feels safe."

If Charles and David ever disagree about a scene, it's usually because of David's comedic long view. "He has great confidence in his sensibility," says Charles. "And over and over he's right.

This page: Director Larry Charles on the set of *Curb*. **Opposite:** Director Bryan Gordon on set with Larry David.

He's a very patient person when it comes to comedy. He's so confident of where he's going that he's willing to throw away laughs along the way because they will distract or diffuse or undermine the laughter he's really going for."

ANDY ACKERMAN

When *Curb* was starting, David asked former *Seinfeld* director Andy Ackerman if he'd like to direct some episodes. After years of working behind the camera with David on *Seinfeld,* Ackerman was impressed by how comfortable he was in front of it. "You know at all times that he's doing the right thing," says Ackerman. "He plays everything so real, and he's such a good actor." As a director, Ackerman tries to give *Curb* more of a film look. "I have a sense that my episodes are a little more polished-looking than the others," says Ackerman. But beyond that, Ackerman says he mostly just sits back and enjoys the show. "They get some really good people, and it's impressive to watch them work," says Ackerman. "There's nothing to tweak, it's pure performance."

BRYAN GORDON

Larry David also met Bryan Gordon working on *Fridays.* As a director, Gordon brings the opposite of Charles. "If there's any quality I contribute it's that I give him a little softness that he doesn't have in other shows," says Gordon. "Larry's a wonderful actor, but he doesn't like touching." After 25 years of friendship, Gordon says David has moved into the hug with him, but that "it's an awkward hug."

Gordon says that *Curb* has taught him how to listen. "I direct a lot of television, and shows like *The West Wing* require knowing the script really well," says Gordon. "But directing *Curb* is all about paying attention every second, because you are writing the show on its feet. Larry is in it, and we're outside of it, and we have to protect him as much as we can.

"Larry is very much this guy from Brooklyn who has his own sensibility and that's what makes him such a genius. Larry will only go to certain Yankee ballgames, and when he calls me up to go out to dinner he's much more interested in the parking than the food. Certain people will melt and compromise, but he hasn't, and there's a lesson to be learned from that."

STORYBOARD: Season Four, Episode 10: Opening Night

"Rose and I went down to see him acting, and when it was all over I said to Rose, 'He'll never make it.'" MORTY DAVID

FAMILY AND FRIENDS: Morty David, Ken David, and Richard Lewis

MORTY DAVID

Larry David's father, former condo president Morty David, was the basis for Jerry Seinfeld's dad, Morty, on *Seinfeld*. He lives with David's mom, Rose, in Fort Lauderdale, Florida, and remembers Larry's childhood with affection:

Larry was a good kid. He was always very cooperative. Never gave us any problems. He was not outstanding, but he was a leader among his friends. They always did whatever he wanted. He would think of something to do and they would all follow. He was always thinking of something to do a little different.

He wanted to go away to college and we sent him to Maryland and he did very well in Maryland. We got him an old car, and he used to travel back and forth every two weeks.

He had a great bar mitzvah when he was 13. He didn't want it, but we had it in a very nice place at the time, the Elegante on Ocean Parkway. We were upstairs and we had all his friends.

When he got out of Maryland he says, "I want to be an actor." We paid for him to go to school to do it. This is a story I never tell anybody, but he was there for less than four months and he tells us he's in a play. So Rose and I went down to see him acting, and when it was all over I said to Rose, "He'll never make it."

I remember when he started going out to the clubs. He used to come home and tell me about this comedian and this other comedian. He kept on plugging along, but he would never take any money from us. I don't know whether he borrowed money, but I think if he emceed he'd get $25 for the night.

Larry was out in California with Laurie and he calls us one day. He's on the plane going to Vegas. He's going to get married. And I said, "Why don't you wait for us?"

Shelley Berman [who plays Larry's father] is wonderful. And the episode when Larry was dancing and singing with Mel Brooks was some show. I thought it was the best thing he ever did.

There were a lot of nice incidents with Larry. Nothing very serious or wrong. I like the way he contributed to the Democratic Party. We made him a Democrat, so that's all right.

KEN DAVID

Larry David's older brother, Ken David, is a computer consultant and investment advisor who lives in Bend, Oregon, with his wife and kids. Though they shared a room growing up, it still came as a complete surprise when his brother told him he wanted to become a comedian.

DO YOU REMEMBER LARRY BEING FUNNY?
Nothing. Zero. But you gotta remember he was four and a half years younger than me. He wasn't that loud and boisterous as a kid. He wanted to go out and have a good time, like any other kid.

Opposite: Larry David, age 12, with his father; David with his parents and brother.

Larry was quick. He was the athletic one, and I was the smart one. Really bizarre, you know?

DO YOU REMEMBER HIM DOING ANY IMITATIONS?
I remember him doing this thing with Bing Crosby, "B-b-b-buddy boy." And I said, "How'd you do that?" And he said, "I put on a tape and listened and talked until I got it."

DID YOU GET ALONG?
Yeah. We shared a room. We watched a lot of *Bilko*. And we watched the Yankee games together at night. Everyone else was a Dodger fan. I always went against the grain.

SO YOU WERE SURPRISED WHEN HE STARTED DOING STANDUP?
When he started doing standup I thought, This is funny. I remember I was watching Richard Lewis on Johnny Carson one night and he talked about his friend Larry David who he said was the funniest guy in the world. And I thought that was great of him. Larry would spend his days writing and then go out at night and perform. I used to worry about him making a living.

HAVE YOU SEEN ALL OF *CURB*?
I don't have HBO. Laura [David's assistant] sends me the tapes. When Larry won the first Golden Globe, he brought the entire cast up and said, "I'd like to introduce these people to my family, who are too cheap to get HBO."

DID YOUR PARENTS WATCH *SEINFELD*?
I'd get a phone call from my mother every Friday morning saying, "Well, what'd you think?" She loved it. There was an episode of *Curb* that Larry forgot to warn them about ["The Special Section," in which Larry's mother dies] that was horrifying to them. I remember being on the phone saying, "Time out! It's not you! This is not real! It's about a fake Larry David. It's not his wife on the show. This is TV, it's either funny or it's not funny." There were things all over *Seinfeld* that came more from their life—Morty Seinfeld's name, the way his hair parted over, the Florida shirts, and the potbelly. It was a tremendous piece of casting. The whole Jewish network was tuned into that show. All the names on the show related to people we know.

BUT *CURB* IS DIFFERENT?
Curb is like grown-up Larry playing around with all his grown-up friends. Watching *Curb* at first I felt like I was watching Larry carrying on a conversation I couldn't answer. I thought Season Four was just genius. When he was working with Mel Brooks I was just jealous.

HOW MUCH LIKE THE REAL LARRY IS THE *CURB* LARRY?

I think it goes in and out. A lot is real, and a lot of that stuff he wouldn't do in a hundred years. He might think about it, but he wouldn't do it. I don't think he would ever be as outrageous personally.

WHAT DO PEOPLE SAY TO YOU ABOUT *CURB*?

There's no ambivalence about it. People either love it or say it sucks. It still strikes me as amazing that they're showing it in Australia. I live in a very non–New York place—Bend, Oregon—and I get a lot of WASP-y type people telling me they love the show. And I'm thinking, Why? What is it about the show that you like? That interests me. I want to know why someone who has blond hair and blue eyes and has been brought up in Lincoln, Nebraska, likes the show. I think the answer is that they see stuff that they might have thought about saying or doing, but never would. That's where it hits them. This guy's got the balls to come out and say what he wants, and do what he wants, and the whole world can piss off.

WAS LARRY AS AWKWARD AROUND WOMEN AS HE CLAIMS?

He was pretty bad with women. Me and the real Kramer always say that a lot of that generation of comics could say anything they wanted to on stage, but get them off stage and it was like, "Ummmmmm." They wouldn't know what to do around anything that was feminine. So Kramer and I had to pull the thorn out of the lion's paw. I wasn't sure Larry would settle down. He had a couple of relationships with nice women, and then he met Laurie and the rest was history.

WHAT DID YOUR MOM DO?

Once we were old enough, she went out and worked as a secretary in the child psych division of the Board of Education in downtown Brooklyn. And every day she'd come home and say, "I told them what you did. Do you know what the psychologists think of you?"

Larry David at 12 years old.

RICHARD LEWIS

Richard Lewis hated Larry David on sight when they met at Camp All America in upstate New York. But when they met again 12 years later at the Improv in Manhattan, they became best friends for life.

WHAT KIND OF 13-YEAR-OLD WAS LARRY?

He was this gangly, aggressive, obnoxious but talented athlete who didn't like the way I guarded him.

WHEN WERE THE TWO OF YOU REINTRODUCED?

Larry denies this, but the first time we met was when he came up to me and said, "Mr. Lewis, can I have a ride across town?" But he will go to his grave denying that he called me "Mr. Lewis." I started doing standup in '71, and Larry came a year after, and we became fast friends. There were 15 or so regulars, and you really had to want it. We used to go from the Improv on the West Side to Catch a Rising Star on the East Side, and the deal was if someone had a car you'd drive everyone back and forth.

DO YOU REMEMBER THE FIRST TIME YOU SAW HIM PERFORM?

I remember I walked into the back of Catch a Rising Star and the first thing I saw was a bit about how he was ill at ease with dating, and how the only way he could conceivably pick up a woman at a bar was to walk in and say, "My name is O'Banion! And I want a companion!" It was dark and funny and twisted and I immediately thought, Anyone who can come up with a premise like that I want to know and become his friend. By that point I never wanted to hear another premise, but I had to see Larry.

DID YOU EVER SEE HIM LOSE IT WITH THE AUDIENCE?

He would storm off the stage. I'm not going to psychoanalyze, but for some reason he wanted undivided attention as a comedian. I would see him storm off when people whispered to the waitress, "We'll have another round." I would always try to lecture him, but he hated to be lectured. He was so purely interested in expressing himself comedically. I remember him telling me about how hard it is to keep the audience's attention for five minutes, and then he started to go a little closer to more traditional standup. It does give a comic more leeway on stage.

David on set with Richard Lewis.

WHEN DID YOU REALIZE YOU KNEW EACH OTHER FROM CAMP?

One night about a year or so into our friendship we were bullshitting and something struck me and it freaked the shit out of me. I looked at him and said, "I think I hate you and I don't know why and I'm scared. I know you from somewhere. You did something really bad to me." He said, "Are you Richard Lewis?" And then we realized we were the two assholes who hated each other from camp. But then we bonded forever. We love each other, but we're so honest that if we get irritated we can turn on a dime.

HOW'D YOU GET INVOLVED WITH *CURB*?

Larry asked me to be in the first hour special and I was. We both love Jack Benny and George Burns and these guys were so close, but in L.A. people don't see each other as much. In the quiet of our own homes I think we realized that the only way we would be able to see each other more often is if we worked together. It came out of a lengthy conversation, but we said, "What can we do?" And Larry came to the conclusion that I could play myself.

IS IT HARD TO PLAY YOURSELF?

At first I was absolutely baffled because what Larry wanted me to do was nothing—just know the outline. That's what's so pure about this show. But it was really hard not to prepare. I would leave the set, and even if Larry was happy I'd have a sense that I had done nothing. I would drive home and think, I think I was funny but I don't know.

IS YOUR CHEMISTRY ON-SCREEN VERY DIFFERENT THAN IT IS OFF-SCREEN?

We're both fearless and argumentative, so when we fight, we really fight. When we're doing a scene, he really covers my ass. I'm not trying to blow smoke up his ass, but the fact is that if I'm going off on a tangent and he thinks I'm undermining my performance, he'll come over and say, "What are you doing?"

WHAT WERE THE EARLY DAYS IN NEW YORK LIKE?

I used to wake him up at three, four in the morning and he would stay on the phone with me, like a suicide hotline. And for a guy who was always talking about how uncomfortable he was dating, he was brilliant at giving advice. As soon as I would call, he'd talk me down. He was one of the people who told me I had to stop drinking. He said, "I think this is causing your problem."

HOW HAS HE CHANGED SINCE THEN?

He would always make faux pas, but they're really just truthfulness. He could be at a funeral and be crying, and notice someone wearing a great herringbone and say, "Where'd you get that?" He was sad, but he also really wanted to know where the guy got the jacket. People didn't always get that, but I think they're starting to see that Larry is just upfront and honest. He's a multitasking neurotic.

As the '80s were drawing to a close, Larry David was living in New York, writing and performing, when his friend Jerry Seinfeld asked him if he wanted to help him work on a TV show for NBC. He immediately said yes, and one cross-town cab ride later, *Seinfeld* was born.

LARRY DAVID: THE *SEINFELD* YEARS

HOW DID *SEINFELD* COME ABOUT?

In 1988 I was performing at Catch a Rising Star when Jerry told me that NBC was interested in doing an hour-long special, and asked if I wanted to work on it with him. Later that evening we shared a cab to the West Side and stopped off at a Korean grocery. We started winding our way through the store and looking at products and talking about them. These were the kind of conversations we had all the time, but it started to sound like good show conversation, the kind we'd never really heard on a TV show before. So that was the seed of it. From there we had a couple of meetings, and it didn't really take very long until these ideas became *Seinfeld.*

WERE YOU AND JERRY PERSONAL BUDDIES OR MORE PROFESSIONAL FRIENDS?

We always enjoyed each other's company and would occasionally go over standup material together. He would tell me stuff he was working on, and I would tell him stuff I was working on.

DID YOU HANG OUT A LOT WITH KENNY KRAMER ACROSS THE HALL?

We were constantly in and out of each other's apartments. He would always drag me along on his errands. If he had to go someplace to pick something up, he'd say, "Come take a ride for 10 minutes." He was very persistent. He'd say, "I've just gotta run into this building to pick up a package." But it was never just 10 minutes, it was more like 40 minutes, and I'd be sitting in the car going crazy and then he'd finally come down and tell me he had one more thing to do. And by the time you got back home it was five o'clock.

DID THE REAL KRAMER EAT ALL YOUR FOOD?

I didn't shop that much for myself, because nobody ever came for dinner. I was so lazy, I hated shopping, and dishes always used to pile up in my sink. So one day I decided to throw everything out and reduce it all to one plate, one knife, one fork, and one spoon, which I recommend for all lazy, single men. But because there was never anything in my apartment, I wanted to be able to go to Kenny's pantry freely without feeling guilty, so I thought the best thing was to pay him for everything I ate. Even if it was one Mallomar. I would figure out how many were in a box and keep track of the percentage I ate. I wrote down everything on a legal pad and would pay him every few weeks. If there was a pint of ice cream and I took a scoop out, I would calculate what I owed him and add it to the list. I wanted no-guilt, refrigerator freedom. I think we did that story on *Seinfeld* too.

WAS THE SHOW YOU PITCHED VERY DIFFERENT THAN THE SHOW *SEINFELD* BECAME?

The show we pitched was about how a comedian gets his material. The idea was to follow Jerry around and see snippets of his life at the dry cleaner, shopping, on a date. And then, at the end of

Opposite: Larry David on the set of *Seinfeld.* **Above:** Kenny Kramer.

the show, to have him do standup based on what we had seen, to show the process of how he had developed his material.

DID YOU PUT UP A FIGHT THE WAY GEORGE DID WHEN HE AND JERRY WERE PITCHING THEIR SHOW ON *SEINFELD*?

Very similar. In fact, at one point I even said, "This is not the show," and everyone looked at me like, Who is this guy? I was responding to the network wanting a three-camera show to be shot in front of an audience. Jerry and I had pitched a one-camera show to be shot on location. So the concept changed dramatically. Elaine wasn't even a character for the pilot, which we shot in '89. We added her when we got picked up for four shows, which we shot in early 1990. They aired them in the summer, the show got picked up for 13 episodes, and I moved to California.

WERE YOU RARING TO GO?

Raring? No, I'm rarely raring. I didn't like the idea of having to move, and I just felt very burdened by the whole thing. I didn't see how I could possibly do it because I didn't have any experience and I didn't know what I was doing. I didn't feel like I had the capacity to write 13 shows, and I remember being pretty disappointed when I heard we were picked up. I felt pressure, and I hate pressure. All my fantasies ended up with me being humiliated.

HOW LONG BEFORE YOU REALIZED YOU COULD KEEP GENERATING NEW IDEAS?

You're never completely confident you have enough ideas for a TV series. It was like when I drove a cab—every time a passenger got out I thought it was my last fare. There were so many available cabs and I couldn't imagine where all the people who needed cabs would come from. In fact, no one person could generate enough ideas to do a TV series. I had plenty of help.

WHY DID YOU DECIDE TO LEAVE *SEINFELD* IN 1996, BEFORE IT ENDED?

I guess I thought it was just time. After seven years I was looking for a new experience.

AND SO THE FOLLOWING YEAR YOU WROTE AND DIRECTED *SOUR GRAPES*?

Yes. Which I thought was a great experience until the movie came out, and then it turned into a not so great experience.

WHAT HAPPENED AFTER IT CAME OUT?

It came out in the spring of '98 and it went away in the spring of '98. The reviews were mixed at best, and, all in all, it was not what I was hoping for. It's so much better to be involved with something that people like. It's difficult if people don't like something you've done.

Opposite: Larry David at a script read-through on the set of *Seinfeld*.

HOW?

I remember when I was on *Fridays*, I'd just bought a Fiat convertible. It was my first job in show business, first time I had a little bit of money, and my first car. I was pretty jazzed. So I was ten minutes out of the dealership, the top was down, and I pulled up at a light and someone at a bus stop yelled out, "Your show stinks!" Well the top went up immediately and it was never down again. The whole experience also creates a lot of tension in your social life. Friends see it and they're put on the spot, because they feel they have to say something nice, even if they didn't like it. It's very awkward.

SO WHAT HAPPENED NEXT?

What happened next was *Curb*.

EVIDENCE: ARTIFACTS FROM THE CURB WORLD

Opposite:
Season 5, Episode 1:
Larry's ill-timed candy grab
This page (clockwise from top left):
S5.E2: Dr Sewell's prescription pad
S5.E10: Casualty of Gentile conversion
S5.E2: Omar Jones's stolen restroom key
S5.E9: Cashew-deficient snack mix
S4.E5: Larry's ski-lift snack
S5.E5: The resurrected 5-wood

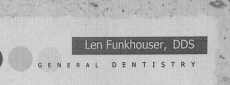

Len Funkhouser, DDS

G E N E R A L   D E N T I S T R Y

9/29/03

Larry David
16294 Winding Way
Malibu, CA 90265

Dear Larry:

Here is a copy of the picture of your tooth for insurance purposes. I have a 8:09 a.m. tee time this Saturday at the club. Hope you can join me. It was a pleasure seeing you again!

Most Sincerely,

Dr. Len Funkhouser

18642 Wilshire Blvd Suite 104   Beverly Hills, CA 90291   USA   Phone: 310.555.4000   Fax: 310.555.4001
Email: Drlen@hotmail.com   Website: Funkhouser.com

CALIFORNIA
DISABLED
PARKING

Dodgers

Sat May 31, 2003
7:10 PM
Season Ticket
BREWERS
46th Season

ADMIT ONE

Dodgers

Sat May 31, 2003
7:10 PM
Season Ticket
BREWERS
46th Season

ADMIT ONE

California

7619E DP

Opposite (clockwise from top left):

S4.E4: Dr. Funkhouser's revenge

S5.E1: Tiny-handled teacup

S5.E3: Squeaky orthotics

S4.E6: Larry's car-pool payment

S5.E3: Susie's nanny-cam bra

S5.E2: Contested permits

This page (from top):

S5.E10: Nat David's eyeglass frames

S3.E4: Life-saving sponge cakes

COFEY
PHARMACIST

Emergency Surgery Performed to Reattach Hand
Dr. Leaves Seder to Perform the Surgery

By Lee H. Vine
for the Los Angeles News

LOS ANGELES-A man trimming his tree fell off of a latter yesterday and cut off his hand just above the wrist. Luckily his friend was able to bring the hand to the emergency room so that it could be re-attached. Dr. Sidney Levine had to preform emergency on the patient immediately. Dr. Levine was called away from his family's Passover Seder to preform the surgery. The patient is doing well, thanks to Dr. Levine, and is expected to regain full use of his hand with only a slight loss of sensation in his fingers.Luckily his friend was able to bring the hand to the emergency room so that it could be re-attached. Dr. Sidney Levine had to preform emergency on the patient immediately. Dr. Levine was called away from his family's Passover Seder to preform the surgery. The patient is doing well, thanks to Dr. Levine, and is expected to regain full use of his hand with only a slight loss of sensation in his fingers.Luckily his friend was able to bring the hand to the emergency room so that it could be re-attached. Dr. Sidney Levine had to preform emergency on the patient immediately. Dr. Levine was called away from his family's Passover Seder to preform the surgery. The

emergency on the patient immediately. Dr. Levine was called away from his family's Passover Seder to preform the surgery. The patient is doing well, thanks to Dr. Levine, and is expected to regain full use of his hand with only a slight loss of sensation in his fingers.Luckily his friend was able to bring the hand to the emergency room so that it could be re-attached. Dr. Sidney Levine had to preform emergency on the patient immediately. Dr. Levine was called away from his family's Passover Seder to preform the surgery. The patient is doing well, thanks to Dr. Levine, and is expected to regain full use of his hand with only a slight loss of sensation in his fingers.Luckily his friend was able to bring the hand to the emergency room so that it could be re-attached. Dr. Sidney Levine had to preform emergency on the patient immediately. Dr. Levine was called away from his family's Passover Seder to preform the surgery. The

This page (clockwise from top left):
S4.E7: Bi-racial baby-shower gift
S5.E4: Incriminating nametag
S4.E3: Susie's dominatrix whip
S3.E1: Chet's shirt
S4.E2: Blinding kabob skewer
S5.E2: Mark's Seder alibi
Opposite:
S5.E4: Nursing home bingo boards

season three

EPISODE 1: CHET'S SHIRT

ORIGINAL AIR DATE: SEPTEMBER 15, 2002 **DIRECTOR:** ROBERT B. WEIDE

Larry buys himself a new shirt, and when Ted Danson (a co-investor in their new restaurant) admires it, Larry buys him one, too. But the shirt has a rip in it, and they wind up fighting over whose responsibility it is to return it. To get out of a dinner invitation, Larry lies to his dentist, but when Ted's daughter breaks Larry's teeth swinging at a piñata at her birthday party, the dentist has an opportunity for revenge.

> "I don't own this shirt anymore. If you give someone a shirt, it's their responsibility."
>
> LARRY TO TED, AFTER TED TELLS HIM HE'S RESPONSIBLE
> FOR REPLACING THE RIPPED SHIRT

STARRING

Larry David .... *himself*
Cheryl Hines ..... *Cheryl David*
Jeff Garlin .... *Jeff Greene*

GUEST STARS

Ted Danson .... *himself*
Michael York .... *himself*

FEATURING

Caroline Aaron .... *Barbara*
Chris Barnes .... *Burt Bondy*
Lou DiMaggio .... *investor*
Alan Havey .... *homeowner*
Kelsey Danae Lewis .... *Jill*
Suzy Nakamura .... *assistant manager*
David Pasquesi .... *Dr. Blore*
Seth Schultz .... *salesman*
Jim Staahl .... *restaurant manager*

120

IN THIS EPISODE

- The name of the restaurant Larry invests in is Bobo's. David used the same name in a scene on *Seinfeld*: Elaine was sitting in the office of the psychiatrist she was dating, the phone rang, and the psychiatrist answered, "Yes, Bobo."
- You can see David's mouth curling up at the sides as he tries not to laugh in the scene at the store when Chris Barnes (Burt Bondy) says, "I know you from somewhere but I just can't place it … I think I know you from the 12:15 spin class down at the gym."
- David doesn't like to wear short-sleeved shirts, so when he discovered a shirt he liked by Tommy Bahama that only came in short sleeves, he would buy two of them and have his tailor add sleeves to the first shirt with material from the second.
- The photograph of Chet is actually of *Curb* producer Tim Gibbons.
- Chris Barnes played Jerry's standup friend Richie Appel on *Seinfeld.*
- After this episode aired, Caruso's on Eighth Street and Wilshire Boulevard in Santa Monica got so many calls from people looking for Chet's shirt that they started selling it.
- Chet's shirt is made by Nat Nast.
- Tony Soprano wore Chet's shirt in an episode of *The Sopranos.*
- David named the dentist Burt Bondy after a guy he went to college with.

WHAT THEY WERE THINKING

Caroline Aaron (Barbara): "What's so funny is that I'll go do another job and people who have careers that I lie in bed and dream about will ask me how they can get on this show. I did a movie with Mia Farrow and she was like, 'What can I do to get on?'"

Larry David on the inspiration for the restaurant storyline: "I was always intrigued by how waiters' uniforms get chosen. Sometimes you'll go into restaurants and they'll all have a striped blue shirt on, and I always wonder, Who came up with that idea? How did that happen? How did the tie get picked out? Was it discussed at a meeting? And so for me, that was right in my wheelhouse. I wanted to be in on the decision-making part of that. Then I thought that in the final episode the restaurant can open and get reviewed, which was an opportunity for me to injure the restaurant reviewer's thumbs."

Robert Weide on the inspiration for the shirt argument: "I was admiring one of Larry's Tommy Bahama shirts, and for my birthday he bought me one. But there was a red dot on it. My point of view was that he should take it back, but he thought it was my responsibility. So it turned into this big debate, which was the inspiration for the fight he has with Ted. It was a red stain, but since there was a sweater with a red stain on it in *Seinfeld,* we changed it to a tear. Ultimately I won the argument, and his assistant, Laura, had to deal with it."

EPISODE 2: THE BENADRYL BROWNIE

ORIGINAL AIR DATE: SEPTEMBER 22, 2002 **DIRECTOR:** LARRY CHARLES

Larry buys his first cell phone and calls Cheryl to see if they can have Richard and his girlfriend, Deborah, over for dinner. But a crucial detail—the fact that Deborah is allergic to peanuts—gets lost due to bad reception, and Deborah gets sick when peanuts are inadvertently served. When Deborah won't take any medicine to reduce her swollen face because she's a Christian Scientist, Richard refuses to be seen in public with her at the Emmys, so Larry comes up with a plan to sneak Benadryl into her favorite brownies.

> "My heart is breaking for her big head."
>
> RICHARD TO LARRY, ABOUT HIS
> GIRLFRIEND'S ALLERGIC REACTION

GUEST STARS

Susie Essman	*Susie Greene*
Richard Lewis	*himself*
Joan Rivers	*herself*

FEATURING

Bill Blair	*Christian Scientist*
Anthony Griffith	*Mike*
Jon Hayman	*Chef Randy*
Allison Heartinger	*Allison*
Jeff Kahn	*salesman*
Robin McDonald	*Deborah*
Maria Quinones	*Cheryl's friend*
Diane Salinger	*Deborah's mom*
Julie Welch	*Julie*

IN THIS EPISODE
- Jon Hayman (Chef Randy) was the voice of the Bubble Boy in *Seinfeld*.

WHAT THEY WERE THINKING

Richard Lewis: "Larry and I were standing outside the front door of the house we were shooting in, having a real argument about all sorts of personal stuff. I was name-calling other people, and I forgot that if you don't turn off your mic everyone in the sound department hears you. As I walked into the scene my eyes fell on the TV monitor and I realized everyone had heard me. So Larry and I took this high-energy anger and made it part of the scene. When I finally saw the cut I was ecstatic. It's mind-blowing for me to be able to be in a show where you can be so true to your own feelings."

Jon Hayman (Chef Randy): "Larry called me up and said, 'I have this part but I want you to audition for it.' So I go in and I'm waiting to audition and there was a very funny, very talented actor there called Grant Heslov. We were outside talking and they called me in and I said—and I was being really completely honest—'I'm not trying to talk myself out of a job, but you've got Grant Heslov out there. Why are you bothering with me?' And they said, 'Perfect, you've got the job. That's exactly what this character is.' The whole point is that the chef quits because he's insecure about his abilities."

Richard Lewis: "For this episode I was faxing and calling and bothering the shit out of Larry because I was like, 'How can you not show what my girlfriend looks like?' We were going back and forth on it, and even when we shot it, as funny as the show was, I hoped he wouldn't get heat from the audience. And lo and behold, I was wrong, and it dawned on me that using your imagination can work better. Larry's instincts are astonishing."

DAVIDISM

LARRY TO THE GROUP, WHO IS UPSET THAT HE CAN'T FIX THE TV:

"Why don't we all go upstairs and get under the covers and sob?"

EPISODE 3: CLUB SODA AND SALT

ORIGINAL AIR DATE: SEPTEMBER 29, 2002 **DIRECTOR**: ROBERT B. WEIDE

Larry thinks Cheryl has a crush on her tennis teacher, Brad, who is also an actor in the play *Tony & Tina's Wedding*. A couple refuses to accept the Davids' wedding gift after a year. Larry has to scramble to find a new chef after Randy quits over the peanut allergy fiasco. Larry has a run-in with a saleswoman who thinks he's stalking her. Larry interrupts sex with his wife for the opportunity to test a new stain removal tip.

> "You don't know anything about men if you think that he doesn't want to have sex with you."
>
> LARRY TO CHERYL, ABOUT HER TENNIS COACH AND ACTOR FRIEND, BRAD

GUEST STAR
Ted Danson .... *himself*

FEATURING
Brad Abrell .... *husband*
Carrie Aizley .... *Melanie Loeb*
Daniel Escobar .... *Chef Josh*
Jon Hayman .... *Chef Randy*
Tim Kazurinsky .... *Hugh Mellon*
Thomas Mills .... *policeman*
Geordie Minn .... *waiter*
Laura Silverman .... *saleswoman*
Jim Staahl .... *restaurant manager*
Josh Temple .... *Brad*
Scott Weintraub .... *Ed Loeb*

IN THIS EPISODE

- David based the conversation between Larry and Brad on his own life: "That happened to me at *Tony & Tina's Wedding*. I was in the men's room and one of the guys in the play came up and started talking to me in character and I said, 'You got the wrong guy.'"
- Scott Weintraub, the man who plays the husband who won't accept the wedding gift, teaches acting at David's daughters' school.
- During a lengthy scene in Larry and Cheryl's bedroom it can be seen that the grandfather clock on the wall never changes time.
- The sign in front of the church in which Tony and Tina get married reads, "Pastor Sheehy" after Bill Sheehy, the show's director of photography.
- Cheryl Hines was Josh Temple's (Brad) improv teacher at the Groundlings.

WHAT THEY WERE THINKING

Josh Temple (Brad): "During the first take of the fight in the bathroom, things got a little heated. Bob Weide was directing, and after the first take he goes 'cut,' and it was dead silent because Larry had left the scene. So I'm still standing in there and I'm scared because I don't know if I've really pissed him off. And Bob comes in and says, 'All right, that's way too tense for me and way too tense for the camera. Someone needs to mellow out, and it's got to be Larry.' So when Larry came back in, I was apologizing for taking things too far, but he said everything was fine. I told him I was going to ask him to hand me a paper towel and he goes, 'You should have, you blew a moment, but don't ever ask me to hand you a paper towel.' I'm sorry, but you just don't get opportunities like *Curb*. My background is mostly improv, and that's your Everest right there."

EPISODE 4: THE NANNY FROM HELL

ORIGINAL AIR DATE: OCTOBER 6, 2002 **DIRECTOR:** LARRY CHARLES

Larry convinces a nanny to let him use the indoor bathroom at a pool party at the home of one of the restaurant co-investors, Hugh, but when Hugh later fires her, she shows up at Larry's expecting him to find her a new job. Larry wants to help Richard get into *Bartlett's Familiar Quotations* for coining the phrase "blank from hell," but ruins the chance when he comments on the size of Hugh's son's penis. At a screening of Richard Lewis's HBO special, Larry and Hugh's son get in a fight.

> "She tells me she likes to pet horses. She enjoys a good corndog. She takes baths with her socks on."
>
> CHERYL TO LARRY ABOUT MARTINE, THE NANNY FROM HELL

GUEST STARS

Ted Danson .... *himself*
Susie Essman .... *Susie Greene*
Tim Kazurinsky..................................... *Hugh Mellon*
Richard Lewis.. *himself*
Cheri Oteri .... *Martine*
Michael York .... *himself*

FEATURING

Michael Aquino ....*Hugh Mellon's son*
Lou DiMaggio ....*investor*
Ashly Holloway ....*Sammy Greene*
Brandon Johnson ....*man eating lunch*
Khali MacIntyre ....*bakery counterperson*
Suzy Nakamura ....*assistant manager*
Jim Staahl ....*restaurant manager*
Richard Tibbets.. *worker*

WHAT THEY WERE THINKING

Tim Kazurinsky (Hugh Mellon): "My favorite memory is the screening-room scene where the boy who played my son had to get in a fight with Larry. He didn't want to say anything mean, so I told Larry I would feed him the lines. I kept saying stuff I knew would get cut, for the amusement of the crew, like: 'Is that your nose, or are you eating a bratwurst?' Larry was really enjoying himself. He totally got the kid into it. Why can't they all be like this?"

LARRY IN ACTION:

Larry compliments Hugh's son.

Larry	Kid's got some penis on him. It's pretty good.
Hugh	What are you saying?
Larry	Your son. His penis.
Hugh	What are you saying that it's big for?
Larry	Hey, it's a compliment. What's the big deal?
Hugh	What's the compliment?
Larry	Well how's it bad? He's got a nice big penis, so what?
Hugh	Well I'm not talking about your wife's tits, am I? I mean, this is rude, it's a—
Larry	You could say my wife has nice tits, as long as it's complimentary.

EPISODE 5: THE TERRORIST ATTACK

ORIGINAL AIR DATE: OCTOBER 13, 2002 **DIRECTOR:** ROBERT B. WEIDE

When Wanda tells the Davids a secret about a possible terrorist attack in L.A., Larry tries to get permission from Cheryl to leave town, with or without her. No one shows up at the Braudys' NRDC benefit. Larry can't stop accidentally snubbing Paul Reiser's wife, and does anything he can (including betraying Alanis Morissette, who tells him who "You Oughta Know" was about) to get back in her good graces.

> "It almost seems a little selfish, that you would want both of us to perish."
>
> LARRY TO CHERYL, ON NOT LEAVING TOWN FOR THE TERRORIST ATTACK

GUEST STARS

Alanis Morissette	*herself*
Paul Reiser	*himself*
Martin Short	*himself*
Wanda Sykes	*Wanda*

FEATURING

Amy Aquino	*Susan Braudy*
Linda Bates	*Mindy Reiser*
Robert D'Avanzo	*food server*
Shelly Desai	*Chuck*
Gerald Devokaitis	*Alanis's assistant*
Antoinette Spolar Levine	*Larry's receptionist*
David Levitt	*guitar player*
Nancy Schnoll	*hostess*
Don Stark	*Stu Braudy*

WHAT THEY WERE THINKING

Cheryl Hines: "Everybody wanted to know what Alanis was whispering in Larry's ear, but he wouldn't tell anybody. We were like, 'Did she tell you a name?' And he was like, 'You don't need to know that.' We all had our theories about her song. I'd heard it was about Bob Saget."

Larry David: "If someone tells me not to say anything to someone, I will never say anything to anyone. Ever. Including my wife. That's how I know I'm getting more boring as I get older."

Don Stark (Stu Braudy): "I'd be yelling at Larry, and he'd start laughing, and I'd go, 'What the fuck are you laughing at?' He'd say, 'I'm not used to people yelling at me.' And I'd say, 'Well, when you're worth $20 billion, a lot of people aren't going to express their anger to you on a regular basis.'"

Amy Aquino (Susan Braudy): "They don't tell you anything about the scene until it's about to shoot, and you don't open your mouth until the cameras are rolling. It's a tremendous show for actors—to be able to use all these parts of your mind."

EPISODE 6: THE SPECIAL SECTION

ORIGINAL AIR DATE: OCTOBER 20, 2002 **DIRECTOR:** BRYAN GORDON

Larry gets home from shooting a movie in New York to find that his mother has died and he's missed the funeral. Richard calls Larry an East Indian giver for giving him his mantra (jai ya), and then asking for it back. Larry comes up with a plan to move his mother's grave, and is psyched to discover he can use her death as an excuse to get out of stuff.

> **Larry:** "How's mom doing?"
>
> **Nat David:** "Oh, well, you know how people do."

NAT DAVID, TRYING TO TELL LARRY THAT HIS MOTHER IS DEAD

GUEST STARS

Shelley Berman	*Nat David*
Richard Kind	*Cousin Andy*
Richard Lewis	*himself*
Martin Scorsese	*himself*

FEATURING

George Coe	*general manager*
Tom Dugan	*cop No. 2*
Harry Murphy	*Ed Swindell*
George Pesce	*gangster No. 2*
Joseph Reidy	*assistant director*
Charley Rossman	*cop No. 1*
Adrian Sparks	*gravedigger*

WHAT THEY WERE THINKING

Richard Kind (Cousin Andy): "Originally, the scene when we were digging the grave was not a montage set to music. Larry started hating me and his father, and Jeff started yelling at me, and we were all yelling at each other over his mother's grave. It was absolutely hilarious. The audience missed a great ending to a very funny scene."

Larry David: "The only episode my dad got upset about was the one where my mother died. I think he was upset because my real mom was so frail at the time."

DAVIDISM

LARRY TO CHERYL, OVER BREAKFAST ON THE BACK DECK:

"I like to pretend that I'm deaf and I try to imagine what it would be like not to be able to hear them. It's not so bad."

EPISODE 7: THE CORPSE-SNIFFING DOG

ORIGINAL AIR DATE: OCTOBER 27, 2002 **DIRECTOR:** ANDY ACKERMAN

At a peace-making dinner with Susan and Stu Braudy, Larry refuses to thank Susan for dinner after Stu pays the bill. Jeff is allergic to Susie's German shepherd (a former corpse-sniffing dog who smells a bra buried beneath the restaurant), so Larry comes up with a plan to find the dog a new home. But when Sammy wants the dog back, Larry winds up having to say thank you to Susan after all.

> "It's nice to be affectionate to something German. You don't get the opportunity that often."
>
> LARRY TO JEFF, ABOUT HIS DOG

GUEST STARS

Ted Danson .... *himself*
Susie Essman .... *Susie Greene*
Michael York .... *himself*

FEATURING

Amy Aquino .... *Susan Braudy*
Lou DiMaggio .... *investor*
Kate Flannery .... *cop No. 2*
Ian Gomez .... *bald chef*
Joey Hiott .... *Braudy son No. 2*
Ashly Holloway .... *Sammy Greene*
Bret Loehr .... *Braudy son No. 1*
Leonardo Millan .... *detective*
Suzy Nakamura .... *assistant manager*
Mark Rolston .... *contractor*
Jim Staahl .... *restaurant manager*
Don Stark .... *Stu Braudy*
Charles Wright .... *cop No. 1*
Hunter .... *Oscar the dog*

IN THIS EPISODE

- To get Hunter (Oscar the dog) to focus on where the bra is buried in the restaurant, the dog handler placed a pile of ham underneath the rubber floormat.
- When Larry returns to the Braudys' to get back Oscar, look closely and you'll see David delivering this line to the sky in order to get through the scene without laughing: "How's the, ah, how's the dog working out?"

LARRY IN ACTION

Larry and the investors discuss the restaurant.

LARRY	How come there's no partitions in the bathroom between the urinals?
TED DANSON	Here?
LARRY	Yeah?
TED DANSON	I don't know. I thought we were gonna have that.
MICHAEL YORK	Well...
LARRY	Huh?
JIM SWENSEN	Do we have, is it important? I mean, it looks nice now.
TED DANSON	Yeah, yeah, it's important.
LARRY	We want a little pee privacy, do we not?

EPISODE 8: KRAZEE-EYEZ KILLA

ORIGINAL AIR DATE: NOVEMBER 3, 2002 **DIRECTOR**: ROBERT B. WEIDE

Wanda's fiancé, Krazee-Eyez Killa, confides in Larry that he cheats on Wanda, and later accuses Larry of telling on him. Susie gets mad at Larry for not taking a house tour. Larry tries to replace a sports jacket that he needs for a re-shoot of the Scorsese movie (and that Cheryl threw away), but winds up getting in a fight with the salesman at the store where he finds a replacement.

"Are you my Caucasian?"

LARRY TO KRAZEE-EYEZ KILLA

GUEST STARS

Susie Essman	*Susie Greene*
Martin Scorsese	*himself*
Wanda Sykes	*Wanda*
Chris Williams	*Krazee-Eyez Killa*

FEATURING

Caroline Aaron	*Barbara*
Al Fann	*Wanda's dad*
Guido Grasso, Jr.	*bar gangster No. 1*
Lynn Hamilton	*Wanda's mom*
Windy Morgan	*wardrobe woman*
George Pesce	*bar gangster No. 2*
Joseph Reidy	*assistant director*
Jason Sklar	*salesman*

IN THIS EPISODE

- Chris Williams is Vanessa Williams's little brother.
- Director Robert B. Weide won an Emmy for this episode.
- Williams and his friends from college made up the word "cundela" (which his character uses to mean copasetic) one summer on Martha's Vineyard. "We were trying to make up a word that people would start saying," said Williams. "It's cool that I got to use it 20 years later as an homage to my boys."

WHAT THEY WERE THINKING

Larry David: "Chris Williams was amazing. In the first scene at his and Wanda's engagement party, he took out this piece of paper and told me he wanted my opinion on a new rap song he'd written, which of course I had no idea he was going to do. So I'm hearing this on camera for the first time, how he's going to cut off my dick. Not a bad way to work."

Chris Williams (Krazee-Eyez Killa): "I'm not like Krazee-Eyez at all. I went to Georgetown. But I wanted to be as authentic as I could be, as hard as possible. I have blue eyes, so I put in brown contacts and went unshaven. I had a goatee, earrings, some chains, a wife beater, baggy pants, a 'doo rag with a rough riders hat, and a toothpick."

Jason Sklar (salesman): "I told my parents, who live in St. Louis, to watch the episode. Now my mom is the kind of woman who will say, 'Why do you need to curse? You don't need to curse to be funny on TV.' But my scene is really clean, so I told her to watch it, and she told all her friends, including my rabbi who had bar mitzvah'd me. Of course it turns out it's the most graphic episode ever. Every other word is 'motherfucking.' There's a pubic hair stuck in Larry's throat. I can no longer talk to my old rabbi."

EPISODE 9: MARY, JOSEPH AND LARRY

ORIGINAL AIR DATE: NOVEMBER 10, 2002 **DIRECTOR:** DAVID STEINBERG

Larry finds the Christmas season particularly challenging: He eats Cheryl's home-baked Nativity scene, offends the housekeeper and tries to blame it on Cheryl, and finds it difficult to give the correct tips.

> "You ate the baby Jesus and his mother Mary!" CHERYL'S SISTER BECKY TO LARRY

GUEST STARS

Paul Dooley .... *Cheryl's dad*
Susie Essman .... *Susie Greene*

FEATURING

John Capes.. *wise man No. 2*
Gary Carlos Cervantes .... *gardener*
Jack Gallagher... *doctor*
Ashly Holloway .... *Sammy Greene*
David Koechner .... *Joseph*
Christopher Kriess .... *club member*
Carlos La Camara .... *waiter*
Paul Lieber .... *wise man No. 1*
Kaitlin Olson.. *Becky*
Dyana Ortelli .... *Dora*
Julie Payne .... *Cheryl's mom*
Alexandra Wilson .... *Mary*

136

IN THIS EPISODE

- Cheryl's parents ask Larry what he's getting Cheryl for Christmas and he tells them he's giving her his grandfather's tallis. The joke was Jeff Garlin's favorite in the history of the show: "I said to Larry, 'If you don't use that I will wrestle you,'" said Garlin.

- The line when Larry asks the gardener if he can use the *tu* form with him is based on one of his old standup bits:

  "Well, you seem like a very nice audience tonight. I'm wondering, in case I break into some Spanish or French, may I use the familiar *tu* form with you people? Instead of *usted*? Because I think *usted* is gonna be a little too formal for this crowd. I feel already I've established the kind of rapport that I can jump into the *tu* form with you. That quickly. I'm taking a *tu* liberty with you. I'm gonna use the *tu* form and that's it. You can't talk me out of it. You know Caesar used the *tu* form with Brutus, even after Brutus stabbed him. He said, *'Et tu, Brute?'* and I think that's a little too informal when someone's trying to assassinate you. At that point, perhaps if he used *usted* he would have been better off. But that's Caesar."

DAVIDISM

LARRY TO JEFF:

"There's nothing worse than Jews with trees."

EPISODE 10: THE GRAND OPENING

ORIGINAL AIR DATE: NOVEMBER 17, 2002 DIRECTOR: ROBERT B. WEIDE

A few days before the restaurant is scheduled to open, Larry fires his bald chef after he catches him trying to "pass" in a toupée and later breaks a restaurant critic's thumbs during a heated elementary school dodgeball game. At the grand opening, Larry's given the opportunity to do something nice for someone.

> "Shit, shit, shit-face, fuck, shit, cock-sucker."
>
> THE CHEF OF LARRY'S RESTAURANT ON OPENING NIGHT

GUEST STARS

Shelley Berman	*Nat David*
Paul Dooley	*Cheryl's dad*
Susie Essman	*Susie Green*
Richard Lewis	*himself*
Paul Sand	*Guy Bernier*
Michael York	*himself*

FEATURING

Caroline Aaron	*Barbara*
Ann Allen	*female dodgeball player*
Jennifer Courtney	*Andy's assistant*
Shelley Desai	*Chuck*
Lou DiMaggio	*investor*
Ben Falcone	*clerk No. 1*
Ian Gomez	*bald chef*
Mina Kolb	*Jeff's mom*
Antoinette Spolar Levine	*Larry's receptionist*
June Kyoto Lu	*carwash cashier*
Suzy Nakamura	*assistant manager*
Louis Nye	*Jeff's dad*
Kaitlin Olson	*Becky*
Dyana Ortelli	*Dora*
Adam Paul	*clerk No. 2*
Julie Payne	*Cheryl's mom*
Jim Staahl	*manager*
Paul Willson	*Andy Portico*

- While they were filming the scene in which Larry and Cheryl get stuck in the carwash, David drove over Cheryl's foot.
- According to *Curb* producer Tim Gibbons, David gives preference to the bald when hiring in real life as well: "When I was interviewing for this job I went to meet Larry and he was looking over my resumé and says, 'So the guys at HBO like you?' And I was like, 'Yeah, I've done a few things with them.' And he says, 'You know, you kind of got a leg up on the other guys.' And I'm thinking this is because the guys at HBO like me. And then he points to his head and starts tapping it, and I realized he meant because I was bald."
- Shelley Berman, who plays Larry's father, Nat David, was part of the original Compass Players with Elaine May and Mike Nichols, which later became Second City. Paul Sand and Mina Kolb were both also early members of Second City.

WHAT THEY WERE THINKING

Michael York: "Right from the start, I found myself being rather aggressive and cutting and rude to Larry. I was astonished. It was this sort of free-for-all. I love improvisation. You'll be playing a character, and then suddenly the character's playing you. I don't think you're yourself at all. You've got to be energetic, bigger. I sensed this with Larry. I loved it when his scabrous personality emerged from the pussycat. I've always had these encounters with this very sweet, soft man who leaps into action with this mask. What I love about him is he can say all those things that we can't say, and observe things that we've noticed all our lives but were too polite or well behaved or apathetic to do anything about. It's fantastic."

Richard Lewis: "One great moment was after we were at this restaurant shooting for 18 hours. I went over to Larry and said, 'Can you believe that we're doing a scene with Shelley Berman?' And he looked at me, and all of the show business shit was stripped away, and we were just two teenagers going, 'Are we lucky or what?'"

Shelley Berman (Nat David): "Larry is the hope for new comedy by going back to the basics of what comedy is. Instead of finding humor in our toilets and in our sex, instead of violating all the sensitivities in the world in order to get one stinking laugh, he's able to confess every damn flaw that he has. We look at this guy and we say, 'Aha! That's me!' *Curb* is not formula-funny. It's original and funny, and the reason it's original, incredibly, is because it's retro. Larry's the everyman comedian because he's the everyman jackass. He's the everyman mistaker, the everyman loser, the schmuck in all of us. We all recognize our own cheating, cheapness, lies, and cowardice. The marvelous thing about us is that we're a hell of a lot funnier than 'motherfucker.'"

THE IMPROV PROCESS: SEASON THREE

Scene 1 from "Krazee-Eyez Killa" (Episode 8)
Larry gets to know Wanda's fiancé, a rapper named Krazee-Eyez Killa.

THE OUTLINE

1. EXT. THE WATKINS' HOUSE
We open on a RACIALLY-MIXED party. CHERYL is talking to WANDA and her boyfriend, KRAZEE-EYEZ KILLA. They have some interaction with an OLDER BLACK COUPLE, who are Wanda's parents. During all of this, we keep hearing a popping noise that sounds like a cap gun going off. We then pan to LARRY and find him stomping on packing bubbles. Cheryl approaches Larry and tells him to cease and desist. He then winds up next to Wanda's father and, desperate for conversation, mentions how he once dated a black woman and was quite surprised by some of the negative comments he heard when they went out, but he wasn't phased by it at all. Then Mr. Watkins excuses himself and Larry starts chatting with Krazee-Eyez Killa. Larry asks where he lives, and after going into some detail about its location, Krazee-Eyez Killa abruptly changes the subject and asks Larry if he likes to eat pussy. Larry, a tad thrown by the question, tells Krazee-Eyez Killa that he used to, but now he's too lazy. "It's a lot of work and it hurts my neck. It's a whole to-do." Krazee-Eyez Killa, taking Larry into his confidence, says that he loves Asian pussy. Larry, a little shocked, says, "You mean you used to." Krazee-Eyez Killa says, "Still. No way I can give that up." Now Cheryl approaches. Larry tells her that he has to go to Jeff's new house to pick up a script. Cheryl thought Jeff was in a hotel because of the dog, but Larry explains that he's getting allergy shots now and they're helping.

WHAT WAS ON AIR

KRAZEE-EYEZ KILLA	What's crackin' playa?
LARRY DAVID	How are you?
KRAZEE-EYEZ KILLA	I'm all right. I'm all right. Yeah, yeah, yeah.
LARRY DAVID	Yeah?
KRAZEE-EYEZ KILLA	I'm chillin'. What's up?
LARRY DAVID	Chillin'.
KRAZEE-EYEZ KILLA	What's up, baby?
LARRY DAVID	Just chillin'.
KRAZEE-EYEZ KILLA	Hey, you a writer, right?

LARRY DAVID	Yeah.
KRAZEE-EYEZ KILLA	Um, I wrote some shit this morning. I wrote some shit. You know, I write my own lyrics and shit, you know what I mean?
LARRY DAVID	Yeah, yeah, I know. Yeah.
KRAZEE-EYEZ KILLA	You wanna help me out with it?
LARRY DAVID	Ah-h— I've never written rap stuff, but—
KRAZEE-EYEZ KILLA	That's all right. You know? Let me see what you got.
LARRY DAVID	Okay, go ahead.
KRAZEE-EYEZ KILLA	Let me see what you got. All right? Check this shit out. It's called "I'm Comin' To Get You."
LARRY DAVID	"I'm Coming To Get You," okay.
KRAZEE-EYEZ KILLA	All right? Right. "So you think you're gonna cross me, and mess with my shit? Opening your fucking trap and flapping your lip. Don't fuck with me nigger, you're gonna get dropped. I'll snap off your neck with a crackle and pop." Like that.
LARRY DAVID	Oh, I like the Rice Krispies thing, yeah.
KRAZEE-EYEZ KILLA	You got that shit.
LARRY DAVID	Yeah, yeah, yeah, crackle and pop, of course.
KRAZEE-EYEZ KILLA	You here. You know what I'm s— Yeah, yeah, yeah, yeah. "If you say anything, you'll be me to die, 'cause I'll make you suck my dick, then I'll nut in your eye. I'll stomp on your world as if my name was Godzilla."
LARRY DAVID	Yeah.
KRAZEE-EYEZ KILLA	"I'm coming for you motherfucker, I'm your Krazee-Eyez Killa." You know, and I'm a be like this in the, in the video, like, you know what I mean?
LARRY DAVID	I like it. I got one tiny, little comment.
KRAZEE-EYEZ KILLA	What? What, what?
LARRY DAVID	I would lose the "motherfucker" at the end. 'Cause you already said "fuck" once. You don't need two "fucks." You already got the one "fuck." I would change the "motherfucker" to "bitch." Because the "bitch"—
KRAZEE-EYEZ KILLA	I'm comin' for you bitch.
LARRY DAVID	Yes, because "bitch" is, is a word that you would use to somebody who—who you don't real—who you disrespect. Right?
KRAZEE-EYEZ KILLA	I see, I see now.
LARRY DAVID	Isn't that so?
KRAZEE-EYEZ KILLA	That's— You my dog. You my nigga'.
LARRY DAVID	I am your nigga'. Absolutely.

"If there's a joker on the set, it would definitely be me." JEFF GARLIN

JEFF GARLIN

The idea for *Curb Your Enthusiasm* was hatched over a chicken lunch on the West Side of L.A. in 1999. Comedian-actor Jeff Garlin was meeting with Larry David when the two decided to get something to eat. David had mentioned that he was thinking about returning to standup, and over lunch Garlin suggested he film the process. He even offered to direct it. David liked the idea, but said no to Garlin directing. Instead, he asked him to be an executive producer and play his manager Jeff Greene. It didn't take much to convince him.

DID DAVID EVER CONSIDER HAVING HIS ACTUAL MANAGER, GAVIN POLONE, PLAY HIS MANAGER ON THE SHOW?
Gavin's name didn't come up. We sort of discovered what our dynamic would be right away, and it almost felt like we'd been a comedy team for years.

HOW MUCH ADVICE DID YOU GET ON CHARACTER?
We went with instinct. Sometimes I'll get it wrong, and Larry will say, "Don't do that anymore," but it's not something I'm nervous about. I'm also more than happy to surprise Larry, see what he thinks. In every single scene there are things that surprise him and work, and things that fail.

DO PEOPLE ASSUME YOU'RE LARRY'S MANAGER IN REAL LIFE?
The people who watch our show are really smart. I'd hate to be famous for being on *Hollywood Squares,* just for being famous, because then you get sycophants. The people who come up to me are very smart people. I would say one out of 50 is pretty stupid and might think I was his real manager, but most are pretty great.

YOU DIRECTED "THE THONG," IN SEASON TWO. WHY ONLY ONE EPISODE?
Larry isn't comfortable with people who are on the show directing. He just doesn't like it. He promised me I could direct one, and since I wasn't in "The Thong," he let me do that one. I certainly have more than my creative share of input as executive producer. I directed a movie that I wrote and I enjoyed that, but except for the money I don't know that I would want to direct much television. TV is a producer's forum.

DO YOU REMEMBER LARRY FROM HIS STANDUP DAYS?
When Larry would go on stage it was very exciting because (a) you loved his material and it was so different than everyone else's, and (b) some comics liked the idea that he was going to snap and walk off stage. I didn't want to see that because there was a long period in my career when I was doing that. It took more to make me snap—with Larry all it took was someone chewing gum and looking in the wrong direction. Me, I'd go up with the anger. I got fired a lot because I hated it when people liked the hack act before me. What fascinated me was that

Opposite: Jeff Garlin and Larry David shooting a scene from Season Four.

Larry was a great comedian that I wanted to see. There aren't a lot of guys that made me want to go in the room and watch them.

WHAT IS YOUR ROLE ON THE SET?
If there's a joker on the set, it would definitely be me. That's my job with the crew. I try and keep things as light as I can.

DO CELEBRITIES TELL YOU THEY WANT TO DO THE SHOW?
So many big movie stars have told me that they want to be on the show over the years, and I've told Larry each and every one of them. Our show is not guest-driven, but certainly we've had guests like Ben [Stiller] and David [Schwimmer] express a desire to be on the show. But they have to fit into the concept Larry has already developed.

DO YOU RECOMMEND A LOT OF ACTORS FROM SECOND CITY?
Ironically, the only episode I know of that we didn't have Second City [the Chicago comedy troupe] people in was the one I directed. The truth is, it is very difficult to find the right people to do this sort of work. With standups, 50 percent can do it and 50 percent can't; with actors, 25 percent can do it and 75 percent can't. When it comes to improvisers there's a certain few who have the style of the show inherently in them.

WHAT'S THE DIFFERENCE BETWEEN TV LARRY AND REAL LARRY?
In real life Larry thinks those things and doesn't say and do them, and on the show he says everything he thinks.

HOW HAS BEING A PART OF CURB CHANGED YOUR LIFE?
The only thing I have to say is that I'm lucky, I'm really lucky. This show has given me a career. I'll work the rest of my life because of this show. I am truly blessed and lucky. Big time.

AN INTERVIEW WITH GAVIN POLONE, THE INSPIRATION FOR JEFF GREENE

The real-life basis for Jeff Greene's character is David's former manager Gavin Polone. As executive producer of *Curb*, Polone says he does "pretty much nothing" on the show, and that aside from some deal-making he's insignificant to the process.

HOW DID THE SHOW COME ABOUT?

The special combined real standup and interviews with some improvised sequences. As the show developed, it became clear to me and to Larry's agent, Ari Emanuel, that this could be a series. Larry didn't have that in his mind, but he was not closed off to the idea. Ari and I told Chris Albrecht and Carolyn Strauss at HBO that they should do it as a series.

WHEN THE SHOW GOT PICKED UP FOR SERIES DID YOU HAVE TO TALK LARRY INTO DOING IT?

I would not say that we had to talk him into it. He enjoyed doing the special. It is just that he had not been intending to do something like this.

WHAT KIND OF CLIENT WAS LARRY DAVID?

He was great in the sense that he is a genius and fun to be around. He was a drag in that he doesn't care about making money, which has a negative effect on the income of the representative. But I was very lucky to have had the opportunity to represent Larry. Truly, it was one of the best things that ever happened to me.

HOW IS JEFF'S RELATIONSHIP TO LARRY ON *CURB* SIMILAR TO YOUR REAL-LIFE MANAGER RELATIONSHIP TO LARRY?

It's about as similar as my physiognomy is to Jeff's. In the beginning there was friction between Jeff Greene and Cheryl David, which may have been loosely based on some difficulty between myself and Larry's wife, Laurie, but that has long since passed. Jeff is more like Larry's Sancho Panza. I can't see any resemblance to my relationship with LD.

WHAT'S YOUR FAVORITE EPISODE?

The last episode of the first year was pretty great. I loved the scene where LD goes to the incest support group and pretends to have been molested as a boy. It brought tears to my eyes. Laraine Newman was brilliant. The irreverence of it was incredibly unique. I don't think anyone has done anything like that before or since. I also loved episode 8 of year 4, where the Native American guy, at LD's behest, tries to help Cheryl with her vaginal problem. That moment when Wandering Bear asks Cheryl "How is your vagina?" is a TV classic.

In 1999, shortly after the release of the movie *Sour Grapes,* Larry David started working on an hour-long special for HBO about his return to standup. The special was a hit, and the network turned it into a series that ran for many years to come.

LARRY DAVID: *CURB YOUR ENTHUSIASM*

HOW DID *CURB YOUR ENTHUSIASM* GET OFF THE GROUND?

I had an office at Castle Rock, and my friend Alan Zweibel had the office next door, and he was writing something for Jeff Garlin. So one day I told Jeff I was thinking about going back to standup, and he suggested I film it. I really wasn't sure I wanted to do it. Finally I talked to my wife about it and she said I should do it. So I said, "Okay, why not?" But as I started thinking about it, the more boring it seemed to me. What would the audience be watching when I was off stage? Was the camera going to follow me into a supermarket? I felt like there needed to be another element. That's when I thought, Okay, I might just make up some stuff. I'll create this story that could take me from on stage to off stage to on stage.

And because I was dealing with standup, I needed a manager. So I asked Jeff if he wanted to play my manager. Then I came up with a story about my wife, about how I would be with this woman in Central Park and run into my wife's friend who would think I was cheating on her, even though the woman I was with was someone I just met. Then I realized that in order for this to work, and to really feel like a documentary, it would have to be improvised. So I asked Bob [Weide] to direct it, because he'd done some documentaries about the Marx Brothers and W.C. Fields and he always loved my act. And he came up with the idea of doing the interview with Jerry [Seinfeld] and some other people. And that's how the whole thing happened.

WHAT TOOK MORE WORK, *CURB* OR *SEINFELD*?

I would say there was probably more stress to the work on *Seinfeld*. Very often we had four days to write, cast, and build sets for a show. On *Curb* I have no writing deadlines.

DURING *SEINFELD* DID YOU EVER THINK IT WOULD BE NICE TO SAY YOUR OWN LINES?

It wasn't a pressing issue for me.

ARE THERE PLACES WHERE IT'S EASIER FOR YOU TO WRITE?

I prefer writing in my office, as opposed to my house. As far as coming up with ideas, I'd say any situation that brings out my immaturity, like a funeral.

WHERE DID YOU GET YOUR ANTENNAE FOR WHAT WORKS AND WHAT DOESN'T?

I don't know, but being from Brooklyn helps. All those families living on top of each other. The lack of privacy, the yelling, the screaming.

Opposite: Larry David on the set of *Curb*.

WHAT COMMENT ABOUT THE SHOW ANNOYS YOU MOST?

People have no compunction about telling me they can't stand it or my character. I went to vote recently and the sweet old woman working behind the table handed me a ballot and told me how much she disliked the show.

WHY DO PEOPLE LIKE *CURB*?

You mean, outside of that woman? I think it's because people see elements in me that they see in themselves and that I'm saying a lot of things they wish they could say. Like if there was a show called *Revenge*, I'd watch it, because I cannot get enough of revenge.

DOES YOUR WIFE OFFER HER OPINION?

Yes, but she doesn't see the shows until they're on the air and by then it's too late.

IS LARRY DAVID IN HIS TWENTIES, LIVING IN NEW YORK, CLOSER TO WHO YOU ARE IN THE SHOW THAN WHO YOU ARE NOW?

Well he wasn't married, and was taking a quart bottle filled with pennies to an all-night grocery and buying Chef Boyardee. But like the guy in the show, he was more of a loose cannon, more apt to get in confrontations with people and more apt to say whatever was on his mind. I'm a lot more censorious now.

WHAT MADE YOU START CENSORING YOURSELF?

Well, first of all, I've experienced some success in my life. That tends to allow you to function much better in society, as opposed to standing on a street corner yelling at people, which was where I was headed.

BUT YOU DIDN'T CARE ABOUT MAKING MONEY.

I wasn't talking about that kind of success. That was never my goal. I just wanted to have enough money to go to the movies and take a cab. To me, if you could live in New York in a one-bedroom apartment and avoid public transportation, you were a success.

WOULD YOU HAVE BEEN CONTENT AS A STANDUP?

I would have been, but somewhere in me I thought, I could do more than just that.

DO YOU HAVE ANY OTHER TALENTS?

When I was doing standup I decided to take piano lessons. So I bought this upright piano, which took up half the space in the apartment. Richard Lewis would come over and I would play Clementi's "Sonatina" for him and he thought I was insane. There are a lot of comedians who are gifted musicians, but I can assure you, I'm not one of them. I feel like I'm a gifted driver and I think it's because I'm so defensive as a person that it works for my driving.

YOU WENT TO COLLEGE IN THE '60S. WHAT ABOUT ROCK MUSIC?

I was quite out of it in the '60s. I couldn't stand marijuana, because whenever I got stoned I would turn into my mother. Or I would go into the bathroom and start berating myself in the mirror, which I did on one of the shows. So I never really felt comfortable sitting with a group of people listening to music. There was also a '60s patois, which I could never get into. How anybody in the world could use the word "groovy" always mystified me. So there was this whole subculture to the music that I felt alienated from, and which, by the way, also included dancing.

HOW DID YOU MEET YOUR WIFE, LAURIE?

She was working on the *Letterman* show and saw me perform one night in the Village. Then, a week later, I ran into her at a restaurant. I waited the requisite three days, then called for a date. The first date we had dinner at a Mexican restaurant, and the second date we went to the beach, which tells you that when I'm trying to get a woman to like me, I'll turn myself into a person I barely recognize. She, unfortunately, was not interested in that person. He was way too accommodating, way too nice, and was incapable of attracting a woman. A third date was not forthcoming.

SO THEN WHAT?

Then a couple of months later we ran into each other on Ninth Avenue. I was eating a plum and the juice was dripping down my face. Very smooth. But I think she felt a little guilty for blowing me off and then after that she made an effort to sort of be friends. My whole theory at that time was that if I developed enough platonic friendships with women, one of them would eventually break. It turned out to be her.

WHEN DID YOU START DATING?

We were both out in L.A. when I was doing the first four *Seinfeld* episodes. She was there producing *Get a Life*. We spent one day together, and I started to feel like she was looking at me in a different way. Maybe it was because I had a job. It's been my experience that women like men with jobs, preferably good jobs. Anyway, when we got back to New York she asked me to walk her home one night, and I wangled my way upstairs.

Above: Larry and Laurie David at an event for the Natural Resources Defense Council.

THE HOUSES

"A lot of weird things happened to *Curb*, but as much bad luck as we ran into, we also seemed to have some sort of guardian angel watching out for us. Wherever we were and regardless of how ill-prepared we'd be, we always magically managed to make whatever needed to happen happen." MICHAEL DIMEO, ART DIRECTOR

Over five seasons of *Curb Your Enthusiasm,* Larry and Cheryl David moved four times, five if you include the special. Of their many moves, only one was voluntary. The rest were the result of the logistical challenge of shooting a TV series on location in L.A. Below, art director Michael DiMeo walks us behind the scenes through *Curb's* game of musical houses.

SEASON ONE
Brentwood, CA

I was not involved with the selection of Larry's house at the beginning of the show. The producers chose an empty house, which turned out to be owned by Sam Raimi (four houses away from the Season Five house). They suggested I take a tour of Larry's real home to get a feel for the way he lived. He's got a giant house, the rooms are enormous, and there are couches in every room, including the kitchen. I was given a very modest budget and only three days to dress this large, empty house before we began filming. I thought to myself, There's no way I'm going to be able to re-create Larry's house on my budget in just three days. We made it look decent but there were certain things that I would never do again. In the master bedroom we used a really dark bed with a leather headboard, and whenever we shot Larry and Cheryl lying in bed talking it always looked like they were in a black void.

The next season rolled around, and the producers decided we needed to make some changes. Larry's wife had come by the set and said that this would not be her house. Since all of our locations other than Larry's house had been real places in the first season, they decided it would be okay for Larry's new house to be a real place as well. It was considerably less expensive for my department.

SEASONS TWO AND THREE
Malibu, CA

This house was more upscale and had a country French shabby chic flavor, which has been a common theme in every season thereafter. We did, however, change certain pieces, because they were white. White is very problematic on video and tends to overexpose, which looks radioactive and blown

SEASON 1 | SEASONS 2 AND 3 | SEASON 4 | SEASON 5

out on TV. This provided an opportunity to transition some of the furnishings from the first house, which also made the "moving" situation more real. This house had a beautiful view of the ocean but the only time you ever saw it was in the first episode of the second season when the Davids buy the house. That baffled everyone. Larry wanted them to live in a nice house, but he didn't want it to be so upscale that he wouldn't appear to be a normal guy. The owners made some changes between seasons so we wouldn't have to move as much of their stuff around for filming. This included a new bedroom set and reupholstering some of the white furniture.

SEASON FOUR
Malibu, CA

We had worn out our welcome at the Season Two and Three house. Filming our show in a real functioning home had taken its toll on the owners and producers alike. We spent several weeks searching high and low for another new house for Larry and ended up at a house that was literally down the street from our Season Two and Three house. We walked in and said, "This is it." We all knew it felt right—the Spanish architecture, the big open rooms, everything about it. We weren't there very often because the show was filming all over town in the build-up to the episode about *The Producers*. But everyone loved the floor plan and the look of the house. We really didn't have to change very much at this location.

SEASON FIVE
Brentwood, CA

This house was down the street from the original Season One house. I was amazed we were allowed back into this neighborhood given the problems we'd had with one of the neighbors during filming of the first season. Larry liked the open floor plan and the big entryway, but wasn't crazy about the owners' furnishings, so we basically gutted it and started over. The house had Spanish architecture similar to the house in Season Four. We added slightly more traditional and contemporary furnishings in contrast to the Eastern/Moroccan flavor of the homeowners' belongings. This time around we had a much bigger budget and more time to make over the house before filming began.

season four

EPISODE 1: MEL'S OFFER

ORIGINAL AIR DATE: JANUARY 4, 2004 DIRECTOR: LARRY CHARLES

In anticipation of their anniversary, Larry reminds Cheryl what she promised him when they got engaged 10 years before, and she gives him the go-ahead to sleep with someone else. Later that night at a karaoke bar, Larry bombs a pick-up, but so impresses Mel Brooks with his rendition of "Swanee," he's offered the lead in *The Producers*.

> "What do you want to be a David for? Davids want to be out of being Davids. I don't want to be a David, I have to be a David. But if you don't have to be a David, why be a David?"
>
> LARRY (IN A FLASHBACK) TO CHERYL, WHEN SHE SAYS SHE WANTS TO GET MARRIED

STARRING

Larry David .... *himself*
Cheryl Hines ..... *Cheryl David*
Jeff Garlin........... *Jeff Greene*

GUEST STARS

Mel Brooks .... *himself*
Cady Huffman .... *herself/Ulla*
Paul Mazursky .... *Norm*
Ben Stiller .... *himself*
Christine Taylor .... *herself*

FEATURING

Philip Baker Hall .... *Doctor Morrison*
Michael D'Amore .... *man in wheelchair*
Rudy De Luca... *Rudy*
Teresa DePriest .... *single woman*
Rachael Harris .... *Joanne*
Lela Lee .... *Bobbi*
Antoinette Spolar Levine .... *Larry's receptionist*
Jeffrey Meyer.. *karaoke MC*
Andrea Piedmonte .... *restaurant waiter*
Lewis J. Stadlen .... *himself/Max Bialystock*
Don Stephenson .... *himself/Leo Bloom*
Tracy Vilar .... *nurse No. 1*

IN THIS EPISODE
- The last school play David did was an eighth-grade production of *Charlie's Aunt*.
- Cheryl gives Larry a free pass to sleep with someone else by their anniversary, which David's wife, Laurie, did for him when he turned 50. "She had complete and utter confidence that nothing would happen," says David. "Not that I wouldn't try, but that no one would be interested."
- Larry chooses karaoke over sex with Cheryl, but in real life David says karaoke is not for him: "It's for normal people. People who don't mind letting others see they're having a good time. I mind."

WHAT THEY WERE THINKING

Larry David: "I was never really any good at the cold pick-up. I couldn't even do it when I had hair. There's no way a bald man can approach a strange woman. The bald man definitely needs an introduction."

Cady Huffman (herself/Ulla): "*Curb* is the greatest place to work. They're all so smart and funny. They're such an assemblage of misfits. They all just sit around and giggle all day long. They were probably not terribly popular in high school, and now they're the most popular kids in school."

EPISODE 2: BEN'S BIRTHDAY PARTY

ORIGINAL AIR DATE: JANUARY 11, 2004 **DIRECTOR**: ROBERT B. WEIDE

Larry comes empty-handed to his *Producers* co-star Ben Stiller's birthday party, then pokes him in the eye with a kabob skewer and refuses to sing "Happy Birthday." Cheryl starts to think Larry's obsessed with breasts. Larry fills the blind rehearsal pianist Michael in on the fact that his girlfriend isn't actually a model. Larry buys one of Susie's studded sweatshirts to give to Ben as a peace offering, but Ben regifts it to Michael, and Susie sees him wearing it.

> "You really have a little ways to go when it comes to dealing with people."
>
> BEN STILLER TO LARRY

GUEST STARS

Mel Brooks	*himself*
Susie Essman	*Susie Greene*
Cady Huffman	*herself / Ulla*
Richard Lewis	*himself*
Paul Mazursky	*Norm*
Ben Stiller	*himself*
Christine Taylor	*herself*

FEATURING

Patrick Bristow	*Steve the choreographer*
Dalton Brooks	*kid at party No. 3*
Ray Buffer	*stage manager*
Jackie Hoffman	*Rhonda*
Ashly Holloway	*Sammy Greene*
Patrick Kerr	*Michael*
Alexandra Korhan	*kid at party No. 2*
Sarah Ann Morris	*Kim*
Devante Warren	*kid at party No. 1*

WHAT THEY WERE THINKING

Larry David: "People are astounded when I tell them I never had a birthday party when I was growing up. Neither did any of my friends. It just wasn't done, and nobody cared."

Jackie Hoffman (Rhonda): "I was in *Hairspray* on Broadway and had signed a contract that said I wasn't allowed to do anything else. So I came up with some cock-and-bull 'family emergency' story and fled in the night. The role was pretty humiliating, but the good part was, no matter how much they uglied me up, Larry said I wasn't ugly enough. I told him, 'That's the nicest thing any man ever said to me.'"

Larry David: "I don't like kabobs. I don't see the point to them. Why are we bothering with a skewer? Why do we have to make this effort with this dangerous stick to get the meat off it? The first bite is easy, you can slide it off with your mouth, but as you get further along you have to use a fork and knife and it's very dangerous. And the whole skewer appetizer? You're stuck with a skewer that you can't seem to get rid of."

DAVIDISM

LARRY TO CADY HUFFMAN, ABOUT BEN'S PARTY:

"Are you so desperate for a party that you have to have a party two weeks after? Wait 'til next year. You missed it."

EPISODE 3: THE BLIND DATE

ORIGINAL AIR DATE: JANUARY 18, 2004 DIRECTOR: LARRY CHARLES

Guilty for causing Michael's breakup, Larry sets him up on a blind date with a Muslim woman. Jeff tells Larry that Cheryl appeared in a sexual fantasy. Larry tries to intimidate a magic trick out of Cheryl's 14-year-old cousin. Larry accuses mentally challenged car washers of stealing his sunblock, and incenses Ben Stiller further when he refuses to move into the front seat when asked.

> "There's something about this middle-aged bald guy that is thrilling!"
>
> MEL BROOKS TO THE OTHER PRODUCERS

GUEST STARS

Mel Brooks	*himself*
Susie Essman	*Susie Greene*
Cady Huffman	*herself/Ulla*
Ben Stiller	*himself*
Christine Taylor	*herself*

FEATURING

J.J. Boone	*woman in house*
Rudy De Luca	*Rudy*
Stanley De Santis	*Stanley*
Judah Friedlander	*Donald*
Rachael Harris	*Joanne*
Patrick Kerr	*Michael*
Joseph Rosenberg	*Joseph*
Gil Santoscoy	*egg thrower*
Earl Shuman	*man in house*
Brad Silverman	*Brad*
Anton Yelchin	*Stuart*
Moon Unit Zappa	*Haboos*

WHAT THEY WERE THINKING

Moon Unit Zappa (Haboos): "Shooting happens really fast, and when there's downtime there's a little unconscious softshoe that Larry does. He hums and sings and whistles. He's like a crazy broken radio that's picking up stations from wherever. He's humming oldies, classical stuff, whatever. It would be the most eclectic radio station on earth."

Susie Essman (Susie Greene): "The crew completely changed toward me when I put on that dominatrix outfit. Men are so visual. These are guys that I had worked with for four years, and all of a sudden they were all, 'Susie, can I get you anything?' They were around me all the time. They were in heaven. Then I changed out of it and back in regular clothes and it was as though I didn't exist."

LARRY IN ACTION

Jeff tells Larry how he fantasized about Cheryl.

LARRY	Do me a favor, okay?
JEFF	What?
LARRY	I don't want you using my wife anymore for that. Okay?
JEFF	I'll never intentionally use your wife for that.
LARRY	What do you mean?
JEFF	You can't control who pops in.
LARRY	Yeah? Okay.
JEFF	You can't.
LARRY	Next time she pops in, pick up your pants and get out of the room.

EPISODE 4: THE WEATHERMAN

ORIGINAL AIR DATE: JANUARY 25, 2004 **DIRECTOR**: ROBERT B. WEIDE

Larry suspects the weatherman is lying about the forecast so he can have the golf course to himself. A photo of Larry's teeth traumatizes Sammy. Larry hurts his back when he falls in the toilet.

> "I didn't say it was a great Hodgkins, it's a good Hodgkins."
>
> LARRY TO HIS DENTAL HYGIENIST

GUEST STARS

Shelley Berman .... *Nat David*
Ted Danson .... *himself*
Susie Essman .... *Susie Greene*

FEATURING

Thom Barry .... *golf starter*
Maria Canals .... *hygienist*
Lou Cutell .... *Leo Funkhouser*
Svetlana Efremova.. *Nina*
Bob Einstein.................................... *Marty Funkhouser*
Ashly Holloway .... *Sammy Greene*
Kathryn Joosten ....*woman at reception*
Gary Kroeger ....*weatherman*
Boris Krutonog .... *Tolie*
Pat LaBorde .... *woman at testimonial*
Alyson Lyon .... *dental receptionist*
Saul Rubinek .... *Dr. Saul Funkhouser*
Ann Ryerson....................................... *Nan Funkhouser*
Don Stark... *Stu Braudy*

IN THIS EPISODE

- David got the idea of "good Hodgkins" from the TV show *Party of Five*, which he used to watch with his wife and niece: "It was a very easy show to get sucked into, and I got totally drawn in."
- Larry tells the dentist, "There are very few subjects I'm an expert on, and I'm an expert on elastic." David has strong feelings on the subject as well: "You cannot take elastic for granted, because the next thing you know, that sock will be off your ankle and your underwear will cease to be effective. Elastic giving out on underwear is not pretty or pleasant."
- David has been obsessed with golf for most of his life: "The first time I played was when I was 14 at summer camp, and I have been addicted to it ever since. This is the one thing I look forward to more than anything else, and I'm terrible at it. I stink at my hobby. There's something incongruous about that."
- In this episode, Ted's dog is named Roxy, which was the name of David's dog growing up.

WHAT THEY WERE THINKING

Gary Kroeger (the weatherman): "Larry and I go back to *Saturday Night Live*. I was the featured performer and writer in the next office. I didn't get a lot of airtime because Larry used me in his sketches and he would never get anything on the show. We knew he was brilliant, but I thought that he had so many demons. I remember thinking, What's going to happen to Larry? Should we all pitch in 10 bucks? Is his bitterness going to implode?"

EPISODE 5: THE 5 WOOD

ORIGINAL AIR DATE: FEBRUARY 1, 2004 DIRECTOR: BRYAN GORDON

After Larry gets suspended from his golf club for a dirty locker, he steals a five wood out of a dead man's coffin and is kicked out for good. Larry's mannerisms are influenced by Steve, the *Producers* choreographer. Larry has a problem with the ratio of raisins to cashews in his new co-star David Schwimmer's father's line of raisins and cashews.

> "I'm not really too worried about the global warming. People like it a little warmer, don't they?"
>
> LARRY TO THE INTERVIEWERS AT THE
> BEVERLY PARK COUNTRY CLUB

GUEST STARS

Bob Einstein	*Marty Funkhouser*
Susie Essman	*Susie Greene*
Paul Mazursky	*Norm*
Saul Rubinek	*Dr. Saul Funkhouser*
David Schwimmer	*himself*

FEATURING

Alan Blumenfeld	*Joe Figg*
Patrick Bristow	*Steve the choreographer*
Maria Canals	*Delilah the hygienist*
Lou Cutell	*Leo Funkhouser*
Ken Howard	*waspy interviewer No.1*
Patrick Kerr	*Michael*
Antoinette Spolar Levine	*Larry's receptionist*
William Ragsdale	*Dr. Anthony Parker*
Jeff Rosenthal	*writer from* Party of Five
Ann Ryerson	*Nan Funkhouser*
Charmaine Shaw-Gil	*nurse receptionist*
James B. Sikking	*waspy interviewer No.2*
Eric Stolhanske	*Sven Jonsson*

162

LARRY IN ACTION

Larry talks to Sven, a golf pro at the club.

LARRY	All right. What is that? Is that Swedish? Sven?
SVEN	It's Norwegian.
LARRY	I'm sorry. I thought Sven was a Swedish name.
SVEN	It's not. Because I don't look Swedish, do I? It's a big difference.
LARRY	Apparently. What's the difference? May I ask?
SVEN	Culture, looks, names, history, food.
LARRY	Okay. Okay. Sorry. Honest mistake.
SVEN	Dancing.
LARRY	Are Swedes touchy if you refer to them as Norwegians?
SVEN	Why don't you ask a Swede?
LARRY	Yeah, maybe I will.

EPISODE 6: THE CARPOOL LANE

ORIGINAL AIR DATE: FEBRUARY 8, 2004 **DIRECTOR:** ROBERT B. WEIDE

Larry decides to pick up a prostitute so he can use the carpool lane to get to Dodger stadium. Nat David's glaucoma is acting up, so Larry buys him some pot, but Marty Funkhouser gets busted for it. Later, Larry gets stoned with his dad, and turns an innocent trip to the bathroom into a showdown.

> "If you're ever looking for a good blow job at a reasonable rate, she's your gal."
>
> LARRY TO THE COUNTRY CLUB INTERVIEWERS WHO BUMP INTO HIM AT THE GAME

GUEST STARS
Shelley Berman .... *Nat David*
Bob Einstein .... *Marty Funkhouser*

FEATURING
Jorge Garcia .... *drug dealer*
Kyle T. Heffner .... *lawyer*
Ken Howard .... *Ken Abbot*
Rod McLachlan .... *defense attorney*
James B. Sikking .... *Jim Remington*
Ed Steidele .... *stadium announcer*
Ken Thorley .... *judge*
Kym E. Whitley .... *Monena*
Marcia Wilkie .... *female juror*

IN THIS EPISODE

- A man named Juan Catalan spent five and a half months in jail on murder charges until his lawyer substantiated Catalan's alibi with footage from *Curb* that showed him sitting near David during the shoot at Dodger Stadium on the day in question.
- Based on Jorge Garcia's performance as a drug dealer in this episode, producer J. J. Abrams cast him in his show *Lost* on ABC.
- Larry David: "Smoking pot was never, ever a good experience for me. Every relationship I ever had would crumble if I ever got stoned. The best part of getting high happened as soon as I started to come down, when I knew I was going to be myself again, a person that I couldn't stand."

LARRY IN ACTION

Larry talks to his stoned self in the bathroom mirror.

AGGRESSIVE LARRY	What are you looking at? You see something? Huh?
MELLOW LARRY	What did I do?
AGGRESSIVE LARRY	You know what you did, you do nothing!
MELLOW LARRY	If you want me to do something just tell me.
AGGRESSIVE LARRY	You've gotta change the diet. I told you about that. I don't want the red meat. You're eating the red meat.
MELLOW LARRY	I'm doing the best I can.
AGGRESSIVE LARRY	Go to a doctor. Get yourself a checkup. Colonoscopy. You afraid to get a colonoscopy? What's a matter with you?
MELLOW LARRY	I'm sorry.
AGGRESSIVE LARRY	Everybody gets it! Get a colonoscopy!
MELLOW LARRY	I'm really gonna do it.
AGGRESSIVE LARRY	Fucking faggot!
MELLOW LARRY	[SPEECHLESS.]
AGGRESSIVE LARRY	You got the father-in-law's birthday coming up. You gonna get a card?
MELLOW LARRY	Okay.
AGGRESSIVE LARRY	You're not gonna get a card. You're not gonna do a fucking thing.
MELLOW LARRY	I'll try and do better, I will.
AGGRESSIVE LARRY	TV, TV, TV, that's what you like to do! Read a fucking book!
MELLOW LARRY	Okay, yeah, you're right. You know everything.
AGGRESSIVE LARRY	Who the fuck do you think you're talking to?!

EPISODE 7: THE SURROGATE

ORIGINAL AIR DATE: FEBRUARY 22, 2004 DIRECTOR: LARRY CHARLES

Larry gets into trouble when he decides to buy a baby-shower gift for the surrogate mother as well as the mom-to-be. At the baby shower, he gets into a conversation with the surrogate about writing and inadvertently causes her to change her mind about giving up the baby. An attractive nurse makes it very difficult for Larry to pass the routine physical exam he needs in order to perform in *The Producers*.

"What's the surrogate etiquette?"

LARRY TO CHERYL

GUEST STARS

Muggsy Bogues	*himself*
Mel Brooks	*himself*
Richard Lewis	*himself*
David Schwimmer	*himself*
Wanda Sykes	*Wanda*

FEATURING

Eric Alexander	*car alarm offendee*
Garcelle Beauvais-Nilon	*Renee*
Elizabeth Beckwith	*surrogate mother*
Eliza Coyle	*Betty Dusenberry*
Jack Gallagher	*doctor*
Mark Griffin	*paramedic No. 1*
Jack Heller	*Irving Schwimmer*
Frank John Hughes	*angry driver*
Thomas Jones	*valet*
Melissa McCarthy	*saleswoman*
Masasa	*nurse*
Jane Piper	*receptionist*
Murray Rubin	*elderly man*
Ryan Yu	*paramedic No. 2*

WHAT THEY WERE THINKING

Wanda Sykes (Wanda): "Larry gets a kick out of me yelling at him and getting in his shit, so I think people enjoy that. I yell at him when he needs to be yelled at. People like that."

Jack Gallagher (doctor): "When I got to the audition, Larry was in the other room making a phone call, but the director told me that Larry and I would be getting into a fight. So when Larry came in the room and said, 'Hi, I'm Larry,' I said, 'Sit down and shut up.'"

LARRY IN ACTION

During his physical for *The Producers*, Larry complains about the waiting-room reading material.

LARRY	What are you doing? Stealing your magazines from garbage cans? I have never seen such a collection of shit in my life.
DOCTOR JACK	All right, we have—
LARRY	They're all like four years old, those things.
DOCTOR JACK	We have other things that we think about other than the magazines. Like giving people medical assistance.
LARRY	*Ladies' Home Journal* from 2001? *People* magazine. Tom Cruise is forty!
DOCTOR JACK	Just keep walking!
LARRY	Emilio Estevez is forty!
DOCTOR JACK	Okay.
LARRY	Wow!

EPISODE 8: WANDERING BEAR

ORIGINAL AIR DATE: FEBRUARY 29, 2004 DIRECTOR: ROBERT B. WEIDE

A *Girls Gone Wild* video comes between Larry and his assistant, who is having trouble getting her job done in the midst of a breakup. Susie suspects Larry had something to do with her dog Oscar's bizarre new behavior. Wandering Bear cures Oscar and also solves the problem that Cheryl's having with her vagina due to sex with an an inside-out condom—the same condom that Larry recommends to his assistant's boyfriend so he'll keep going out with her, and prevent her from quitting.

"How's your vagina?"

WANDERING BEAR TO CHERYL

GUEST STARS
Susie Essman .... *Susie Greene*
Russell Means .... *Wandering Bear*

FEATURING
Charles de Bernier .... *documentary narrator*
Hunter... *Oscar the dog*
Antoinette Spolar Levine .... *Larry's receptionist*
Joey Slotnick .... *Marvin*

IN THIS EPISODE

- *Curb* executive producer Larry Charles's assistant, Tanya Oskanian, describes how she inspired the assistant storyline: "I broke up with my boyfriend of seven years and came to work and was randomly bawling. I was a mess for a week. It got to the point where Larry Charles was getting me coffee and not asking me to do a single thing for him. He told Larry David he thought it would be a good story for Antoinette. I remember standing in the kitchen one day and saying to Larry, 'I hear you're using my story in an episode.' We were literally standing by the water cooler, and he was like, 'This is how I got half my ideas for *Seinfeld.*'"

....

INTERVIEW WITH LARRY DAVID'S ASSISTANT, LAURA FAIRCHILD, WHO HAS WORKED FOR HIM FOR SEVEN YEARS

WHAT WAS YOUR JOB INTERVIEW WITH LARRY LIKE?

Well, Larry was trying to manage his neck and back pain at the time, so he was wearing a magnet around his neck and arms. Then at one point he looked over at his arm and goes, "Uh-oh, I'm bleeding." He called in his assistant and she got him a bandage. He must have picked a scab.

WHAT DO YOU THINK CINCHED IT?

We were shooting at the Playboy Mansion this past season and somebody on the set asked Larry, "What made you want to hire Laura?" And he said: "I sensed discretion."

SO YOU'RE NOT LIKE ANTOINETTE, LARRY'S ASSISTANT ON THE SHOW?

The whole crew calls her the anti-Laura because she is exactly the opposite of who I am. I'm brunette and she's blond. She is always trying to be involved in Larry's life, and I rarely even ask, "How was your weekend?" She's someone who sits at her desk and reads *Modern Bride.*

WHAT IS IT LIKE BEING HIS ASSISTANT?

The first six months were a little odd. When I first started working for him, he said, "This will be the easiest job you'll ever have—you can even get another job." I didn't answer his phone or open his mail. And then slowly I started getting his lunch and running errands. It takes time for him to build trust with someone. Now we are tight about certain things. He likes to say I know more details about him than his wife does, and I guess I do when it comes to his everyday habits. He doesn't use a computer, so I think we bonded while he was writing the shows and had to dictate to me. He'll ask my opinion on sentences, which, to me, is amazing that he cares about my feedback. But we don't have the kind of relationship where he knows what's going on in my life, and I kind of like it that way.

169

EPISODE 9: SURVIVOR

ORIGINAL AIR DATE: MARCH 7, 2004 **DIRECTOR:** LARRY CHARLES

With the deadline to cash in on Cheryl's anniversary present rapidly approaching, Larry gets the okay from his rabbi to sleep with another woman, and then blows an easy opportunity with his Hasidic dry cleaner. Larry mistakenly invites a cast member of the TV show *Survivor* to dinner with his father's friend, an actual Holocaust survivor, and they don't exactly hit it off. The Davids renew their wedding vows.

> ## "It's a go-home stain, but I didn't go home."
>
> LARRY TO THE RABBI, DESCRIBING THE WINE STAIN ON THE SUIT HE'S WEARING TO RENEW HIS VOWS

GUEST STARS

Shelley Berman	*Nat David*
Paul Dooley	*Cheryl's Dad*
Susie Essman	*Susie Greene*
Gina Gershon	*Hannah*

FEATURING

Colby Donaldson	*Colby*
Barry Gordon	*rabbi*
Kaitlin Olson	*Becky*
Julie Payne	*Cheryl's mom*
Eric Poppick	*Shlomo*
Allan Rich	*Solly*

170

IN THIS EPISODE

- It took more time—around 20 hours—to edit the scene at the dinner table in which Solly and Colby get into a fight than it did to edit any other scene in the series.

WHAT THEY WERE THINKING

Gina Gershon (Hannah): "I went wild when we were shooting and had some really rude, raunchy stuff come out of my mouth. It's like you're making some crazy chef salad and Larry will be like, 'Okay, let's try it again, but without the ham.'"

Cheryl Hines: "We shot the limo scene on the run, and it was really hot and we were all crunched in the car together. So we did one take and I spilled wine all over Larry, but then we couldn't find the wardrobe department because they had gotten lost a few miles back. We didn't have another tie for Larry to put on, so he had to buy the tie off the limo driver."

Julie Payne (Cheryl's Mom): "Larry's behavior is completely reprehensible, until you realize he's only reacting to petty offenses the way you would if you gave yourself permission. He won't let anything go. He's Everyjerk."

EPISODE 10: OPENING NIGHT

ORIGINAL AIR DATE: MARCH 14, 2004 **DIRECTOR:** ROBERT B. WEIDE

Larry flies to New York for the debut of the *The Producers*, where he gets in a fight with David Schwimmer over a lost watch and alienates his cousin Andy and about half of the staff of his hotel. He pretends to have O.C.D. so that Cady Huffman will sleep with him, but ultimately fails to make good on Cheryl's anniversary present when, mid-kiss, he notices Cady has a photo of George W. Bush in her dressing room.

> "What are you doing in the lobby 20 minutes before the show fighting with a Sikh?"
>
> CHERYL TO LARRY

GUEST STARS

Anne Bancroft	*herself*
Mel Brooks	*himself*
Cady Huffman	*herself/Ulla*
Richard Kind	*Cousin Andy*
Nathan Lane	*himself*
Paul Mazursky	*Norm*
David Schwimmer	*himself*
Susan Stroman	*herself*

FEATURING

Nelson Ascencio	*room service waiter*
Yvette Brown	*stewardess*
Bill Buell	*drunk*
Kevin Carolan	*bartender*
Herman Chaves	*mugger*
Stephen Colbert	*male tourist*
Maddie Corman	*female tourist*
Cynthia Ettinger	*fellatio teacher*
Maziyar Jobrani	*Sikh*
Zachary Levi	*bellman*
Cindy Lu	*in-flight announcer*
Eric Millegan	*delivery person*
Ira Mont	*stage manager No. 1*
Tessie Santiago	*chambermaid*
William Wise	*newsstand owner*

IN THIS EPISODE

- The couple who arrive at David Schwimmer's hotel room party are played by *Curb* editor and co-producer Jon Corn and Megan Murphy.
- David was inspired to do *The Producers* storyline when he went to see the show in NYC. "I got the idea as I was watching the play. The actors made it look so easy that it didn't seem beyond the realm of possibility that I could play Max Bialystock, and I was quite tickled at the prospect. So I started writing the season and had already written three episodes before I had lunch with Mel and asked him if we could do it. Mel was the one who made it happen, because we needed the full cooperation of the show and the unions. Then, soon after we started filming, I went up to Portland to see the show again, this time knowing I was going to have to do a few of the numbers. As soon as it started, I was mortified. It seemed impossible. It was a classic what-have-I-gotten-myself-into moment. For the rest of the show, I kept thinking about how I could write myself out of it, but it was too late, so I began to learn the dance numbers. The assistant choreographer, James Hadley, came to my basement—he had a lot of patience because I was not a quick learner. But filming that episode at the St. James Theater with the cast of *The Producers* was easily the most memorable experience I had on the show."

WHAT THEY WERE THINKING

Larry David: "Tipping is a bit of an obsession of mine. It requires too much preparation and thought. And it's quite maddening because it has to be done deftly. It's just a terrible, anxiety-producing process. And let's face it, if you have a $20 bill and the tip you need to leave is much smaller, you feel like an idiot asking for change. I feel like if I ran for president on the platform of no tipping, I'd win."

Susan Stroman, director and choreographer of *The Producers*: "When Larry David called to say that he wanted to learn 'King of Broadway' for one of the episodes of *Curb Your Enthusiasm*, it sounded like a joke in itself. Everybody was so excited at the thought of Larry David being on the stage at the St. James, so all the unions came together to make it happen. We began the process of getting him rehearsed. Now as talented as Larry David is, he is not a dancer. However, my goal was to make it look like he could dance in a Broadway show. I had one of my assistants start working with him on the basics. He was fantastic. I think he loved learning a new skill. He really rose to the occasion and had a dogged determination to make sure the choreography was right."

These scenes were improvised based on the following outlines.

Scene 3 from "Mel's Offer" (Episode 1)
Larry proves to Jeff how inept he is with women.

THE OUTLINE

3. INT. KARAOKE BAR

Karaoke party is in full swing. There are a few celebrities present, and singing onstage is none other than Mel Brooks. Larry runs into Jeff, who's surprised to see him there. Larry tells him how Cheryl offered sex in lieu of the party, but he turned it down. "Same woman for ten years," Larry says. "Can't compete with karaoke." Larry then tells Jeff about the 10th anniversary sex deal. They're amazed Cheryl's even considering it. Larry says that if she agreed, he probably couldn't go through with it anyway. There's also the small issue of who the woman would be. Jeff suggests someone from his past. Larry says if he was going to do this, it would have to be with someone he's never been with—otherwise, what's the point? Larry then sets out to demonstrate for Jeff just how inept he is with women by stopping one and striking up a conversation, which goes nowhere. Larry now gets asked to sing. He tries to get out of it, but he's dragged to the stage area. He then picks up a microphone and launches into an inspired rendition of Al Jolson's "April Showers" with some choreography thrown in as well. Everyone's quite impressed by the performance—none more so than Mel Brooks.

WHAT WAS ON AIR

LARRY DAVID	Do you wanna see, you wanna see how inept I, I really am?
JEFF	I wanna see you in action, inept.
LARRY DAVID	Yeah? You wanna, do you wanna see this?
JEFF	Go, go, yeah, go, go make a move. Show me. Just practice. I'll watch. Go ahead.

Larry walks over to a woman.

LARRY DAVID	Do you like karaoke?
WOMAN (giggles)	Yeah.
LARRY DAVID	It's good, you know. Something to do at night. There's nothing to do at night. What can you do at night? Bowling, movies. It's like a third thing to do after bowling and the movies. I don't know if you bowl or not, I don't go that often—
LARRY DAVID (CONTINUED)	But it's fun, it's fun. You can't find a ball. That's the problem.

LARRY DAVID (CONTINUED)	I don't know why, maybe you own a bowling ball. I don't own a bowling ball. My whole life every time I'm in a bowling alley sticking my fingers in all these holes, picking up the balls.
LARRY DAVID (CONTINUED)	You gotta get your own ball. I don't bowl enough to think to get my own ball.
LARRY DAVID (CONTINUED)	It takes up a lot of space in the house. You keep looking at it in the closet going, "What am I doing with a bowling ball? You don't even bowl!" You know what I mean? So you don't wanna get rid of the ball. How do you get rid of a bowling ball? Think about that. Who do you give a bowling ball to? Nobody bowls. The thing is it only fits your fingers. You throw a bowling ball in the garbage can—you know what the sanitation man's gonna do? He's going to knock on your door. That's how upset he's going to be. He's going to say, "Who the fuck—" (LAUGHS) "threw a bowling ball in the garbage can?"
LARRY DAVID	Okay. All right.
LARRY DAVID	I'm around town.
MEL BROOKS	[Mel sings lyrics to "Just in Time."]
JEFF	How'd it go?
MEL BROOKS	[Mel continues singing "Just in Time."]
ANNOUNCER	Come on ladies, put 'em together for Mel Brooks. How about that? That was fantastic. Great, now who wants to go next? Huh? Anyone? Huh, hey, Larry David.
LARRY DAVID	Oh, come on.
ANNOUNCER	What do you say, Larry? Can you come up and do a song?
LARRY DAVID	Ahh, come on, stop it. Huh? Nah, no. Uh, come on, listen, no.
ANNOUNCER	Come on Larry.
LARRY DAVID	You gotta be kidding me. Are you crazy? Oh, please stop. Oh, you people, come on. For me? No, I can't do it.
ANNOUNCER	You too shy for this?
LARRY DAVID	All right! Ahh, shut up. Come on. All right. All right.
LARRY DAVID	[Larry sings opening lyrics to "Swanee."]

Scene 5 from "The Blind Date" (Episode 3)
Larry won't move up to the front seat.

THE OUTLINE

5. EXT. YOGA CLASS
Ben drops his wife off and asks Larry to move up front. Larry says they're less than five minutes from the rehearsal hall and it doesn't make much sense. Ben insists. Larry doesn't want to. They continue the argument as Ben drives off.

WHAT WAS ON AIR

BEN STILLER	Why don't you come up front?
LARRY DAVID	Ehh.
BEN STILLER	Hmm?
LARRY DAVID	I'm okay.
BEN STILLER	Come on up front.
LARRY DAVID	I'm good. I'm good.
BEN STILLER	Are you serious?
LARRY DAVID	Yeah, why? What's the difference?
BEN STILLER	Larry, I'm not gonna drive you around like I'm your chauffeur. Get in the fucking front seat, all right?
LARRY DAVID	Ben, you're not driving me around like I'm a chauffeur. We're two minutes from, from the rehearsal hall.
BEN STILLER	You know, w-what kind of person asks another person to drive them around like this? This is the kind of mentality is what's—
LARRY DAVID	What, what, what kind of person is so insecure that they have to make somebody move into the front seat so they don't think that they're driving somebody around?
BEN STILLER	No, the kind of person that's so insecure that needs to be driven around in the backseat, subliminally, you're telling me, that you need me to drive you around?
LARRY DAVID	That has nothing to do with me being driven around. Why do I have to leave my seat, go into the front seat—
BEN STILLER	Because I asked you to sit in the front seat of my car and it's my car and if, uh, it's my car, I make the rules, okay?
LARRY DAVID	It's a—Ah, now you're making the rules? Yeah. We w-

	would have already been there already. Oh yeah, very good, very good.
BEN STILLER	Yeah, very good, very good. Yes, we would have already— Very good.
LARRY DAVID	Oh, you can't drive with somebody in the backseat?
BEN STILLER	Yeah, you're such a baby. You're a, a—You're a grown man baby.
LARRY DAVID	I-I'm not a—Are you saying I'm a man-child?
BEN STILLER	I'm saying you're a little baby. And I'll g— You know what, little baby wants a ride? We'll give little baby a ride.
LARRY DAVID	Oh, you know what, I'm— Little baby, wants to walk. Yeah. Little baby's gonna walk.
BEN STILLER	No, no, no. No, no, no. Little baby— No. No, you know what? I should have brought my little baby seat for my, for my— No, no.
LARRY DAVID	No, no. The little baby's gonna walk.
BEN STILLER	Mr. David, where, where to now?
LARRY DAVID	Oh, won't you—
BEN STILLER	Where to now, Mr. David?
LARRY DAVID	Oh, and if I didn't read the rules getting into the car?
BEN STILLER	Here we go. Driving Mr. Larry.
LARRY DAVID	Hey. Hey, take it easy, man.
BEN STILLER	You're the baby, Larry.
LARRY DAVID	Oh, I'm the what? I'm the baby. What?
BEN STILLER	Yeah. You're the baby.
LARRY DAVID	Why? 'Cause I wanna take a poll, that makes me a baby?
BEN STILLER	No, because you're—No, you know what makes you a baby? The fact that you're a big stupid baby.
LARRY DAVID	Well then—What? What? Oh, I'm a big stupid—L-look at this thing you're walking around with. A big shack on your back.
BEN STILLER	Yeah, and—What? It's a, my knapsack.

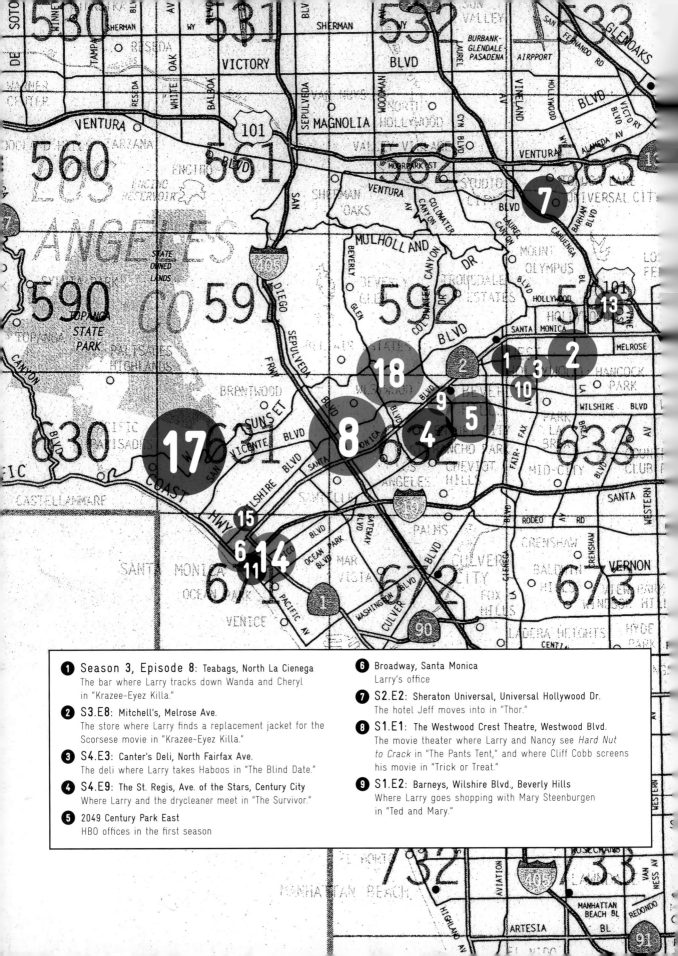

1 **Season 3, Episode 8:** Teabags, North La Cienega
The bar where Larry tracks down Wanda and Cheryl in "Krazee-Eyez Killa."

2 **S3.E8:** Mitchell's, Melrose Ave.
The store where Larry finds a replacement jacket for the Scorsese movie in "Krazee-Eyez Killa."

3 **S4.E3:** Canter's Deli, North Fairfax Ave.
The deli where Larry takes Haboos in "The Blind Date."

4 **S4.E9:** The St. Regis, Ave. of the Stars, Century City
Where Larry and the drycleaner meet in "The Survivor."

5 2049 Century Park East
HBO offices in the first season

6 Broadway, Santa Monica
Larry's office

7 **S2.E2:** Sheraton Universal, Universal Hollywood Dr.
The hotel Jeff moves into in "Thor."

8 **S1.E1:** The Westwood Crest Theatre, Westwood Blvd.
The movie theater where Larry and Nancy see *Hard Nut to Crack* in "The Pants Tent," and where Cliff Cobb screens his movie in "Trick or Treat."

9 **S1.E2:** Barneys, Wilshire Blvd., Beverly Hills
Where Larry goes shopping with Mary Steenburgen in "Ted and Mary."

THE MAP

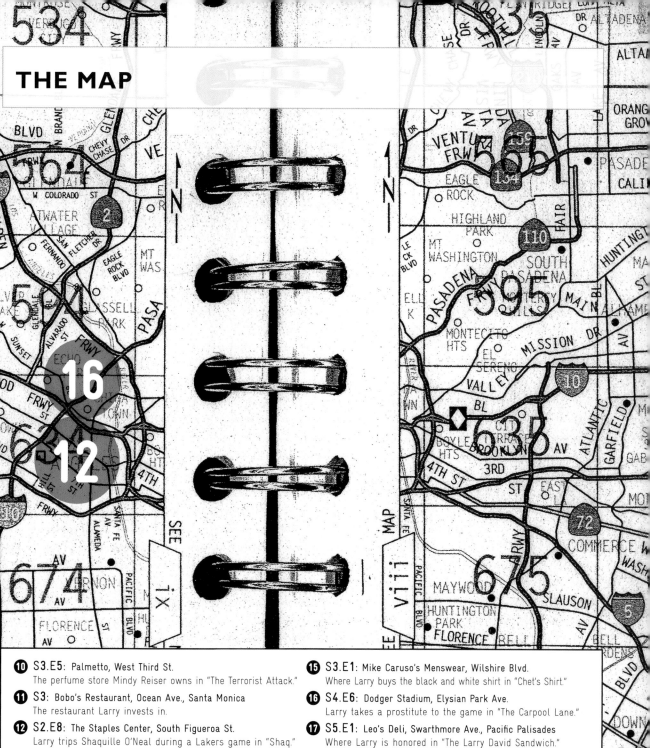

10 **S3.E5**: Palmetto, West Third St.
The perfume store Mindy Reiser owns in "The Terrorist Attack."

11 **S3**: Bobo's Restaurant, Ocean Ave., Santa Monica
The restaurant Larry invests in.

12 **S2.E8**: The Staples Center, South Figueroa St.
Larry trips Shaquille O'Neal during a Lakers game in "Shaq."

13 **S2.E1**: Toyota of Hollywood, Hollywood Blvd., Hollywood
Where Larry works in "The Car Salesman."

14 **S3.E4**: Butterman's, Pico Blvd., Santa Monica
The bakery where Larry buys the sponge cake
in "The Nanny From Hell."

15 **S3.E1**: Mike Caruso's Menswear, Wilshire Blvd.
Where Larry buys the black and white shirt in "Chet's Shirt."

16 **S4.E6**: Dodger Stadium, Elysian Park Ave.
Larry takes a prostitute to the game in "The Carpool Lane."

17 **S5.E1**: Leo's Deli, Swarthmore Ave., Pacific Palisades
Where Larry is honored in "The Larry David Sandwich."

18 **S5.E6**: The Playboy Mansion, Charing Cross Rd., Beverly Hills
Larry and Wilson visit the Playboy Mansion in "The Smoking
Jacket."

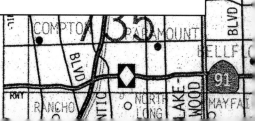

"There are a lot of takes because of Larry's laughing, which is joyous in a way. I start yelling at him and he starts laughing immediately, so I kind of know the minute I start yelling that he's going to laugh. He starts to laugh before I even begin to speak."

SUSIE ESSMAN

SUSIE ESSMAN

Larry David only had one thing in mind when he started searching for an actress to play Jeff Greene's wife, Susie: she would have to curse convincingly. He'd known standup comic Susie Essman for years, but it wasn't until he saw her roasting Jerry Stiller at a Friar's Roast on Comedy Central that he realized how well she knew her way around a four-letter word. "I thought, Boy, what a mouth on this girl," said David, who had already written the outline for the scene in "The Wire" (Season One) in which Susie curses out Jeff for getting them robbed. He called her up and offered her the part without bringing her in to audition.

When not filming *Curb,* Essman (whose speaking voice is the only thing in common with her TV alter ego) lives a mellow life on Manhattan's Upper West Side. That is, until she gets a few blocks down Broadway and someone hands her a phone and demands she call her husband a fat fuck.

WHY DO PEOPLE GET SUCH A KICK OUT OF SUSIE?

People always talk about the language that she uses, but I have a theory that it has nothing to do with the swearing. I think it's her complete and total comfort with her anger. That resonates with people because so many people, especially women, are afraid of their anger. Susie is completely reactive and in the moment. There's no self-reflection. She never thinks, Well, maybe something else could be happening. Larry says something, Jeff says something, and she reacts.

HOW DID HER CHARACTER EVOLVE?

Well, she's not like me at all. In the first season I think I was in three episodes, the first of which really just introduced my character. But then in the episode with the Fresh Air Fund kid ["The Wire"] Larry said, "Don't hold back, I want you to rip Jeff a new asshole." Little did he know what he was unleashing. He walked into the house to play computer golf with Jeff and I said to him, "What the fuck do you want?" And he lost it. He just lost it. We had to do that take so many times because he kept losing it.

HOW MUCH DIRECTION DOES LARRY GIVE YOU?

Sometimes he'll say, "Add a fuck, take away a fuck. Less angry, more angry." Usually I'll play it at a certain level and then ask him if he wants more or less, but it's never off by that much. Sometimes it's affected by whether or not he's coming off a scene in which somebody else is already screaming and yelling at him. At this point, there's definitely an intense dialogue of the unconscious going on. There's a trust there. It has to be like that when you're improvising. Sometimes after we do a take, especially if I've been particularly harsh, he'll come over to me like he just smelled shit and I know what he's going to say and I just say, "Okay."

IS SUSIE BASED ON ANYONE?

She's a composite of several different people in my life. She's a rich Beverly Hills housewife and a

Opposite: Susie Essman on set with Cheryl Hines and Larry David.

mother who will protect her children at all costs. Everything is an indignity to her. She doesn't have a job. In Season Four she had the shirts she was selling out of the trunk. She believes that she has incredible taste. But a lot of what she gets angry about is justified—Larry got her kid drunk, stole her dog, stole her doll's head. I can go a little over the top in the anger, but it's totally justified. She's not just angry and screaming and yelling at nothing. Larry's acting like an asshole most of the time.

WHAT KIND OF RESPONSE DO YOU GET ON THE STREET?
People are nuts. The response I get from a lot of women, especially from married, suburban housewives, is that I'm their idol. Susie says everything they want to say to their husbands. A lot of women tell me, "My husband tells me I'm exactly like you. We watch you and my husband says, 'That's you!'" I think a lot of women identify with the frustration and anger of dealing with these morons that I have to deal with. Sometimes they want me to tell their husbands off. They'll hand me a phone and say, "It's my husband, call him a fat fuck." I've done that for charity before, when someone paid about $2,500 at an auction for me to create an outgoing message on somebody's machine that said, "Leave a fucking message."

WHAT ABOUT MEN?
There are so many men that are turned on by Susie, especially the sado-masochists. They just want me to scream and yell at them. Certain men are scared of it, and others are completely turned on by it, which just makes me laugh. I've always had a huge following of gay men as a standup.

I find that often people are disappointed when they meet me. They don't like that I'm a somewhat normal human being who speaks in a normal way and am not telling them to go fuck themselves all the time. I can visibly see the disappointment on people's faces. It's called acting. But it's true for all of us. Cheryl is nothing like her character. None of us are really like our characters.

ON AVERAGE, HOW LONG DOES IT TAKE FOR YOU TO GET THROUGH A SCENE?
Sometimes it'll just be magic and everything will happen on the first take, but usually it takes us a bunch of takes before we find the scene. A lot of times it's just logistical information that has to be gotten out. Larry is focused on story, which is why the improvising works so well. It's not haphazard slapdash improvising. In each scene we know what information needs to be conveyed, but sometimes it takes a while before we figure out the right order and how we want to pull the scenes together. And then there are always problems with laughing.

WHO LAUGHS THE MOST?
Larry breaks the most. There are a lot of takes because of Larry's laughing, which is joyous in a way. I start yelling at him and he starts laughing immediately, so I kind of know the minute I start yelling that he's going to laugh. He starts to laugh before I even begin to speak. It's a thirty-minute show, but we might spend 15 minutes on a scene that will have to be cut down to three minutes.

DO YOU HANG OUT WITH JEFF WHEN YOU'RE NOT FILMING?

Jeff and I are good friends. We get along really well. He'll come to New York and we'll go out and people freak out when they see us together. We'll be at a restaurant, and they can't believe that combo platter. One night we went to a Knicks game and people were shouting out from the stands, begging me to curse them. "Yo Susie! Call me a fat fuck! Tell me to go fuck myself!" For some reason when we're out together it's more than people can bear. One time Jeff was in Bloomingdale's and a woman came up to him and said, "I just saw your wife at Barneys."

WHAT'S LARRY LIKE ON SET?

Working with Larry is an absolute dream. He's a pleasure for people to work with because he's so clear and direct. He's also not Mr. Stroke. He's focused on what's going on and he's not thinking about what you need. You have to be an adult to work with him. I know how much Larry loves me and loves what I do, but I don't hear it that often. If you're a needy actor, forget about it.

Larry is never tired and cranky. He's always focused. I think writing the outlines is torture for him, but once we're shooting he's in heaven. It's pure joy to him. I read the outlines at the beginning of the season—and I have a comedian's brain—and I have no idea how he got there. His brain is something that I can't decipher and that's the definition of genius. I know whatever he gives me is going to be funny. It's a blessing and a curse, because I'll never do anything as funny as this.

season five

EPISODE 1: THE LARRY DAVID SANDWICH

ORIGINAL AIR DATE: SEPTEMBER 25, 2005 **DIRECTOR**: ROBERT B. WEIDE

Larry has a near-death experience swimming in the ocean and decides he wants to go to temple for the High Holy Days, even if he has to buy scalped tickets. Leo's Deli names a sandwich after him, but he hates the ingredients, and it causes his dad to have a stroke. In the hospital, Nat tries to tell Larry something, and Larry thinks it might be that he's adopted. It's the best news he's heard in years.

> "The only noticeable thing I have in common with them, honest to God, is my penmanship."
>
> LARRY TO JEFF, ON THE NEWS THAT HE MIGHT BE ADOPTED

STARRING

Larry David .... *himself*
Cheryl Hines ..... *Cheryl David*
Jeff Garlin .... *Jeff Greene*

GUEST STARS

Richard Lewis .... *himself*
Ted Danson .... *himself*
Shelley Berman .... *Nat David*
Susie Essman .... *Susie Greene*
Kenneth Kimmons .... *Dr. Sewell*
Ed O'Ross .... *Leo*

FEATURING:

Paul Ben-Victor .... *ticket scalper*
Galvin Chapman .... *Graham*
Rabbi Morley Feinstein .... *rabbi*
Crista Flanagan .... *Mrs. Seiderman's nurse*
Jay Frailich .... *Cantor*
Mary Gillis .... *Mrs. Seiderman*
Charlie Hartsock .... *sitcom actor*
Tracy Howe .... *security guard*
Susan Mackin .... *Graham's mother*
Jamie Elle Mann .... *sitcom actor*
Kimberly Page .... *doctor's girlfriend*
Tami Sagher .... *waitress*
Robb Skyler .... *man at temple*
Lynne Marie Stewart .... *nurse in Nat's room*
Veronica Welch .... *woman at party*

WHAT THEY WERE THINKING

Richard Lewis: "It took an hour and a half to shoot the scene in the synagogue when I'm jealous of Larry having a sandwich named after him. Larry said it was one of the funniest things we've ever done. I was really focused on being angry, and every time I would stare at him he would lose it. I was so proud. There's nothing better than to make Larry laugh."

LARRY IN ACTION

Larry answers the phone while having sex with Cheryl.

CHERYL	Get off.
LARRY	What?
CHERYL	Get off of me.
LARRY	What are you doing?
CHERYL	What am I doing? What are you doing?
LARRY	Huh? Yeah. What? What's the— What's the big deal? What?
CHERYL	Why'd you have to answer the phone?
LARRY	Cause I told you I was expecting a call. Why? So what? I mean—
CHERYL	Jesus. Good night.
LARRY	Oh right. Mustn't interrupt the intercourse. Oh sacred intercourse, cannot be interrupted. Ooh, everybody be quiet, quiet for intercourse. Ssh, don't disturb the intercourse.

EPISODE 2: THE BOWTIE

ORIGINAL AIR DATE: SEPTEMBER 25, 2005 DIRECTOR: LARRY CHARLES

Larry hires a private investigator to find out if he's adopted, gets in a fight for using a disabled bathroom stall, tries out the bowtie look, offends a group of African-Americans, gets a racist dog, and loses his status as a man lesbians love when he gets too excited about Jodi Funkhouser no longer being gay.

"Lesbians love me."

LARRY TO JEFF

GUEST STARS

Bob Einstein .... Marty Funkhouser
Susie Essman .... Susie Greene
Mekhi Phifer .... Omar Jones

FEATURING

Mayim Bialik .... Jodi Funkhouser
Curtis Brengle .... band member
Craig Cackowski........................... man No.1 in bathroom
Josh Cooke .... Dan
Michael D'Amore .... man in wheelchair
Fido .... Sheriff the dog
Jim Gleason .... man No.2 in bathroom
Terry Halvorson .... band member
Sue Kolinsky .... Sue
Troy McKay .... man No.3 in bathroom
Melissa Paull .... waitress
Gerry Pineda... band member
Markus Redmond .... loud man at party
Ann Ryerson .... Nan Funkhouser
Steve Seagren .... handyman
Amir Talai .... waiter
Larry Thigpen .... handyman No.2
Tom Virtue .... man with stutter
Wendy Yuponce .... band member

188

WHAT THEY WERE THINKING

Michael D'Amore (man in wheelchair): "I'm actually in a chair in real life and when we were shooting the scene in the bathroom Larry kept saying 'the able-bodied person's stall.' And I finally said, 'Larry, someone's going to nail you on this, you're going to get letters if you use that expression.'"

Mayim Bialik (Jodi Funkhouser): "Bob Einstein is one of the funniest people I've ever spoken to. We'd had a long day filming the anniversary party, which included a lot of extras having to dance all day and look like they were having a good time. And all day long Bob had running commentary. He would pick out a couple and start imaginging out loud what was going on in their heads. It really kept the filming from being boring."

LARRY IN ACTION

Larry misunderstands Cheryl.

CHERYL	Larry, we need to talk.
LARRY	It's over?
CHERYL	What's over?
LARRY	The marriage?
CHERYL	Why would our marriage be over?
LARRY	W—you said we needed to talk.
CHERYL	Yeah, we need to talk about Marty Funkhouser's party.
LARRY	Oh. (Sighs.) Okay.

EPISODE 3: THE CHRIST NAIL

ORIGINAL AIR DATE: OCTOBER 9, 2005 DIRECTOR: ROBERT B. WEIDE

Larry gets a new pair of noisy but comfortable orthotics, and then convinces his housekeeper to tell her boyfriend, Jesus, to get a pair. Cheryl tells Larry to get the housekeeper into a bra or she's history. Larry's orthotics ruin the secret of the Tooth Fairy for Jeff and Susie's daughter, Sammy. Susie catches Larry on video dancing around with one of her bras. Larry steals a *Passion of the Christ* nail from around his sleeping father-in-law's neck to nail a mezuzah to the front door jamb.

> "I knew there was no Tooth Fairy even before my teeth fell out."
>
> LARRY TO SUSIE

GUEST STARS

Paul Dooley	*Cheryl's dad*
Susie Essman	*Susie Greene*
Shelley Berman	*Nat David*
Julie Payne	*Cheryl's mom*

FEATURING

Lydia Blanco	*Maria*
Lydia Cornell	*bra saleswoman*
Ashly Holloway	*Sammy Greene*
Carlos Jacott	*podiatrist*
Lobo Sebastian	*Jesus*
Hunter	*Oscar the dog*

IN THIS EPISODE

- David got the idea for the bra plot when he saw his wife's bra and decided to take a look. "While I was looking at it I thought, This is very funny. I didn't have any idea what my wife's bra size was until I wrote this episode."
- During editing David couldn't decide if the bra conversation with his housekeeper was funny, so he asked a random selection of women from surrounding offices to screen the episode and tell him what they thought: "Once you give them permission to be critics they'll start thinking like critics and make their complaints."

WHAT THEY WERE THINKING

Lydia Blanco (Maria): "My parents were in town to see a play and came to visit on set. My dad's a Catholic deacon, so it was really awkward. Larry pulled me aside and asked, 'Are you comfortable?' I was like, If they want to leave, they can leave. So there I was, braless with a crew of guys, and I was a little worried it was going to scar my parents, but they were too starstruck and excited that I was working on something to really care."

DAVIDISM

LARRY TO CHERYL'S DAD, ABOUT CHRISTIANITY:

"I'll worship a Jane, but, you know, to worship a guy, it's a little gay isn't it?"

EPISODE 4: KAMIKAZE BINGO

ORIGINAL AIR DATE: OCTOBER 16, 2005 DIRECTOR: ROBERT B. WEIDE

Larry forces a Japanese art dealer named Yoshi to lose face after he grills him about his kamikaze pilot father who happens to live in the same nursing home as his father. At a poker game with Yoshi's brother-in-law the next night, Larry is up a lot of money when they get a call that Yoshi tried to commit suicide (after sending a suicide group email). Larry thinks his father's girlfriend, Ruthie, is cheating at bingo. Yoshi's kamikaze pilot father takes a run at Larry in his electric wheelchair.

> "I say to you, they are not kamikaze pilots. He *grazed* the ship. That sounds to me like, I think I might head home, this is fucking insane."
>
> LARRY TO KEVIN NEALON, ABOUT YOSHI'S DAD

GUEST STARS

Kevin Nealon .... *himself*
Shelley Berman .... *Nat David*

FEATURING

Matt De Caro .... *Dr. Skadden*
Ann Guilbert .... *Lenore*
Elanie Kao .... *Miyuki*
Alan Kirschenbaum .... *poker player No.1*
Victor Kobayashi .... *sushi waiter*
Kenji Nakamura .... *sushi chef No.1*
Angela Paton .... *Ruth*
Philip Rosenthal .... *poker player No.2*
Lew Schneider .... *poker Player No.3*
Louisa Springs .... *nursing home resident*
Ken Takemoto .... *Tanaka*
Toshi Toda .... *sushi chef No.2*
Greg Watanabe .... *Yoshi*
David Wells ....*pharmacist*

IN THIS EPISODE

- At a BBQ restaurant in Santa Monica David saw the words "Cofey was here" carved into a table and wondered what kind of an idiot would do that.
- David used to play a lot of bingo at his mother's nursing home: "I never won, but like I say on the show, I always felt like I was going to."
- David says the scene in which he tells the doctor to find out if the bingo game is fixed is the silliest scene he's ever done.
- During editing, David realized the sound from the porn movie his father was watching wasn't clear enough. He asked one of the show's PA's, Charlee Halphen, if she would dub some porn audio for them, and she nailed it on her first try. When they screened her scene later, it received one of the biggest responses that season.

WHAT THEY WERE THINKING

Kevin Nealon: "Just being in a scene with Larry was sort of surreal. It was very awkward for me because I don't swear in real life. The director and producers would come up to me and say, 'You should say something like, "What the fuck is going on here?! This is bullshit!"' It was really difficult to keep a straight face. We came very close to having to shut down the episode."

Ken Takemoto (Tanaka): "Losing face is a very true experience. My parents used to say, 'Whatever you do, remember the effect of your actions. The neighbors are going to know and we're all going to lose face, not just you.' It's a Japanese culture thing. They have a saying, 'If there's a nail sticking up, pound it down, so that everybody is the same.' You never want to stand out and be different."

EPISODE 5: LEWIS NEEDS A KIDNEY

ORIGINAL AIR DATE: OCTOBER 30, 2005 **DIRECTOR**: ROBERT B. WEIDE

Larry locks himself out of his car and, while waiting for Jeff to pick him up, convinces a guy named Pete to drive him through the Jack in the Box (which won't serve him on foot). Richard Lewis needs a kidney transplant, but his cousin Louis Lewis won't donate his organs until he dies, so Larry and Jeff Eeny-Meany-Miny-Mo over who should give Richard a kidney. Pete is arrested for murder and calls Larry to be his alibi.

> "We're losing the sickness and health clause. I'm out if anything's wrong with you. And look, same for you, you go too, okay? I can't be around illness. It freaks me out, okay?"
>
> LARRY TO CHERYL, ABOUT GETTING SICK

GUEST STARS

Richard Lewis	*himself*
Bob Einstein	*Marty Funkhouser*
Susie Essman	*Susie Greene*
Mekhi Phifer	*Omar Jones*
Frank Whaley	*Pete Hagen*

FEATURING

Timothy Brennen	*police detective*
Claudia Cohen	*woman in line*
Nicole Randall Johnson	*Omar's receptionist*
Mindy Kaling	*Richard Lewis's assistant*
Suzanne Kent	*nurse*
Kelvin Han Yee	*newscaster*

JEFF IN ACTION

Richard Lewis's nurse tells Larry and Jeff they're both compatible for a transplant.

Jeff	Goodnight nurse.
Nurse	Goodnight.
Jeff	It's just a saying.
Nurse	I never heard of it.
Jeff	It's an old one.
Nurse	That's nice.
Jeff	It is.
Nurse	I know it is.
Jeff	Do you?
Nurse	Do you?
Jeff	I do.
Nurse	Good for you.
Jeff	It is good for me.
Nurse	Oh you think so?
Jeff	I know so.
Nurse	I'm glad.
Jeff	So am I.
Nurse	That makes two of us.
Jeff	So you say.
Nurse	So I did.

195

EPISODE 6: THE SMOKING JACKET

ORIGINAL AIR DATE: NOVEMBER 6, 2005 **DIRECTOR:** DAVID STEINBERG

Larry's wish for Louis Lewis to die sort of comes true (he's in an irreversible coma) and he visits him intending to pull the plug, but when Louis's 13-year-old room-mate Wilson busts him, Larry promises to fulfill Wilson's dream of seeing a naked woman by bringing him to the Playboy Mansion with Jeff and Andy. When they arrive, Larry ends up scaring away all the naked women in the grotto and gets into a smoking jacket mix-up with Hef. For his birthday, Cheryl arranges for Larry to play golf with Gary Player.

> ## What happens to the mustache in a coma?
>
> LARRY TO THE DOCTOR, ABOUT LOUIS LEWIS

GUEST STARS

Shelley Berman	*Nat David*
Hugh Hefner	*himself*
Richard Kind	*Andy*
Bobbi Sue Luther	*Bobbi Sue*
Holly Madison	*Holly*
Bridget Marquardt	*Bridget*
Gary Player	*himself*
Kendra Wilkinson	*Kendra*

FEATURING

Trisha Debski	*social worker*
James Pickens, Jr.	*doctor*
Grant Rosenmeyer	*Wilson*
Bill Saluga	*Louis Lewis*
Rhett	*Oscar the dog*

IN THIS EPISODE

• *Curb* rented the Playboy Mansion for $15,000.

• Hugh Hefner was anxious about appearing on the show until he found out that a group of Playboy bunnies were big fans.

LARRY IN ACTION

Larry and Louis Lewis's doctor talk beside the comatose patient.

LARRY	So how long do you think he has?
Doctor	It's hard to say. It could be days, weeks, months, um, there's been cases where patients have been in comas for years.
LARRY	Oh, really?
Doctor	Yeah. Yeah.
LARRY	What do you think you're leaning more toward? Weeks or months?
Doctor	Uh, it's hard to say. Uh—
LARRY	If you had to pick one.
Doctor	Un, I don't know if I could pick one.
LARRY	Uh, take a shot.
Doctor	No.
LARRY	Well. You know what happens to the mustache in a coma?
Doctor	The mustache?
LARRY	Yeah, his mustache.
Doctor	Um, it continues to grow. There's a lady who comes in a couple times.
LARRY	Really? The hospital has a barber?
Doctor	Yeah. She's a nice lady. She clips his mustache, she does his hair.
LARRY	She just works within the hospital, or—
Doctor	Within the hospital, yes. Uh huh. We just try and keep him comfortable.

EPISODE 7: THE SEDER

ORIGINAL AIR DATE: NOVEMBER 13, 2005 DIRECTOR: ROBERT B. WEIDE

Larry suspects a cosmetic surgeon friend named Mark of stealing his newspaper and invites some of his neighbors from across the street to his Passover seder so they can identify him. A sex offender moves into the neighborhood and he and Larry hit it off, so Larry invites him to the seder, too. At the seder, the sex offender tells Larry he saw Jeff's conservative brother-in-law tell his son where Larry hid the matzoh.

> ## "Oh boy, look at the Jew girl."
>
> LARRY TO CHERYL, WHILE SHE'S COOKING
> PASSOVER DINNER

GUEST STARS

Shelley Berman .... *Nat David*
Susie Essman .... *Susie Greene*
Robert Corddry .... *Rick Leftowitz*

FEATURING

Emily Charouhas .... *Emily*
Lisa Gerstein .... *Susie's sister*
Pat Harrington .... *Mac*
Ashly Holloway .... *Sammy*
Rob Huebel .... *Mark*
Lauren Katz .... *Marla*
Jacob Price .... *Jacob*
Austin Rogers .... *Stevie Dunkel*
Karly Rothenburg .... *Carol*
Stephen Tobolowsky .... *Len Dunkel*
Jennie Ventriss.. *Ethel*

198

IN THIS EPISODE

● Larry and Jeff use a hand wiggle to represent "conservative" in this episode. David says he was hoping the move would catch on.

WHAT THEY WERE THINKING

Rob Corddry (Rick Leftowitz): "You can definitely see how *Curb Your Enthusiasm* has evolved from *Seinfeld,* and I think it's much more sophisticated. TV today has to be grounded in reality, and *Curb Your Enthusiasm* is hyperreal. In the age of reality shows I guess that's what comedy becomes."

DAVIDISM

LARRY TO HIS NEIGHBORS:

"You never see people drinking grape juice."

ORIGINAL AIR DATE: NOVEMBER 20, 2005 **DIRECTOR:** LARRY CHARLES

Richard Lewis is getting sicker by the day and tries to guilt Larry into donating his kidney. Meanwhile, Larry is waiting for Louis Lewis to die and become the donor. Larry runs into George Lopez, who tells Larry that with a little ass-kissing, the head of a kidney consortium can be gotten to, so Larry befriends him by crashing into his car, leaving a note claiming responsibility, and pretending to be an Orthodox Jew.

> ## "These big vagina ladies are getting away with murder."
>
> JEFF TO LARRY, AFTER RICHARD'S NURSE, AN OLD GIRL-FRIEND, ACCUSES HIM OF HAVING A SMALL PENIS

GUEST STARS

Richard Lewis	*himself*
Susie Essman	*Susie Greene*
George Lopez	*himself*
Mekhi Phifer	*Omar Jones*

FEATURING

Iris Bahr	*Rachel Heineman*
Mo Collins	*Lisa Thompson*
Stuart Pankin	*Ben Heineman*
James Pickens, Jr.	*doctor*
Bill Saluga	*Louis Lewis*
Jim Vickers	*stunt coordinator*

IN THIS EPISODE

- This episode of *Curb* was Lopez's first job after his real-life kidney transplant. When David mentioned to him on a phone call that Alonzo Mourning had dropped out, Lopez told him he'd love to do the show, and David rewrote the outline to accommodate him.
- *Curb* assistant art director Lisa Thompson offered to let David use her name for the nurse who has the big vagina.

WHAT THEY WERE THINKING

George Lopez (himself): "Larry is just like a Zen comedy master, so being on the show is like being in the Chicago Bulls uniform, playing with Michael Jordan. I knew they worked without a script and I'm a comedian for 25 years so I thought, Shit, I can handle a little improv. You just open your mind. It's like a really expensive car, it's meant to run fast."

Iris Bahr (Rachel Heineman): "In the show, Larry tried to fool my character into thinking he's a mega Jew, but having gone to an Orthodox school as a child, I didn't buy any of it. At one point we got into a heated debate about religious law and in an attempt to catch him at his ignorance I asked him 'What does the Mishnah say about this issue?' He replied in full confidence:

Larry: The Mishnah? He says—
Iris: He?!
Larry: She???
Iris: It!!!"

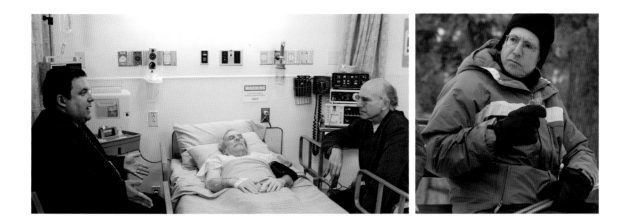

ORIGINAL AIR DATE: NOVEMBER 27, 2005 **DIRECTOR:** BRYAN GORDON

The Davids' friends Mark and Marla have an engagement BBQ on the beach, and Marla helps herself to the fleece jacket in Larry's car and then stains it with s'mores. Larry's misery over a lost sports bet is misunderstood as sympathy when Jeff's dog Oscar gets sick eating Oreos. After his Korean bookie admires Oscar, Larry suspects him of kidnapping the dog and serving him for lunch at Mark and Marla's wedding, where he runs into a post-boob job Rachel Heineman.

> Larry: You go around calling Jeff a fat fuck.
>
> Susie: Jeff is a fat fuck, Oscar's just big-boned.
>
> LARRY TO SUSIE, AFTER SHE YELLS AT HIM FOR CALLING OSCAR FAT

GUEST STARS
Susie Essman .... *Susie Greene*

FEATURING
Iris Bahr .... *Rachel Heineman*
Rob Huebel .... *Mark*
Lauren Katz .... *Marla*
Bobby Lee ....*Sang*
Stuart Pankin .... *Ben Heineman*
Rhett .... *Oscar the dog*

IN THIS EPISODE

- David's friend Bobby Kelton told him a story that inspired the storyline about being fake upset about Oscar the dog: "There was a comic named George Miller who passed away. He was a friend of mine, and he was kind of ill. And one night I was watching the Giants/Angels World Series and the Giants blew the World Series and I was out of my mind, and ten minutes later I get a call and I have to rush down to Cedars-Sinai hospital. I'm sitting outside intensive care and my head's in my hands and I'm not looking up and it's all because the Giants have blown the World Series, not because my friend had emergency brain surgery. All these doctors were asking how I was doing— little did they know what I was really bummed out about."

WHAT THEY WERE THINKING

Iris Bahr (Rachel Heineman): "They gave me those silicone cutlets to wear for my boob job, and I had to get the okay from Larry, who kept wanting them bigger. So I'd put two more in. At one point I had six in and my boobs were jutting out two feet from my body. I had no idea how massive they had become until I saw the crew photo and finally realized why everyone in the crew was smiling at me so much that day. Needless to say, at the end of the day when I took them out I felt severely inadequate."

Bryan Gordon (Director): "I actually feel that it's to Larry's credit that he doesn't shy away from who he is. The way he treats religion is relentless. As much as he makes fun of other cultures, he makes fun of Judaism. I think he really respects the culture. He's a satirist; he's able to surgically skewer every religion."

DAVIDISM

LARRY TO THE KOREAN BOOKIE:

"You know the Three Little Pigs? One built his house with bricks. I'm the pig with the bricks."

ORIGINAL AIR DATE: DECEMBER 4, 2005 **DIRECTOR:** LARRY CHARLES

Louis Lewis comes out of his coma, and Larry finds out he's adopted and travels to Bisbee, Arizona, to meet his birth parents. Larry soon figures out the "Cohens" are actually Cones, and starts fishing, drinking, and going to church, where a sermon on friendship moves him to head home and give his kidney to Richard Lewis. After the operation, Larry is surrounded by loved ones when he dies and goes to heaven. He likes it in heaven, but when he starts fighting with the guides, they decide he's not ready and send him back to life.

> ## "Oh my god, I'm Gentile."
>
> LARRY TO HIS "BIRTH" PARENTS

GUEST STARS

Dustin Hoffman	guide No. 1
Sacha Baron Cohen	guide No. 2
Bea Arthur	Larry's mother
Richard Lewis	himself
Susie Essman	Susie Greene
Shelley Berman	Nat David
Mekhi Phifer	Omar Jones

FEATURING

Tennie E. Barnes	townsperson No. 1
David Lee Fayram	townsperson No. 2
Pat Finn	car owner
Jack Gallagher	doctor
Bob Glouberman	Matt
Barry Gordon	rabbi
Susan Griffiths	Marilyn Monroe
Wallace Langham	man in bathroom
Robert Pine	Ben Hogan
Craig Robinson	attendant No. 1
Hansford Rowe	Mr. Cone
Bill Saluga	Louis Lewis
June Squibb	Mrs. Cone
Beth Tapper	nurse
Neil Vipond	pastor
Julius Wilson	townsperson No. 3
Susan Yeagley	stewardess

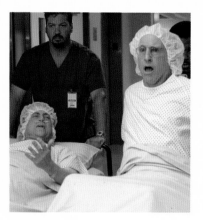

WHAT THEY WERE THINKING

Dustin Hoffman (guide No. 1): Hoffman was going to play himself in the first *Curb* episode, but ended up bowing out because he was uncomfortable with the idea. Hoffman told David that if he wrote a part for him that wasn't him, he'd be happy to do it. "My kids were upset with me for not doing it," said Hoffman. "They said, 'How can you turn down Larry? It's the best show!'"

LARRY IN ACTION

On a flight, Larry wants out of the emergency row.

LARRY	Uhm, listen. I can't really sit here, by the emergency door exit. I think you better get someone else.
Stewardess	Okay. Sir, we're about three minutes from wheels up. So you need to just stay put okay? Because we've got a full plane.
LARRY	Okay, no, no, no, no. You don't understand. I can't be sitting here if something happens. I can't, we won't be able to get out.
Stewardess	Calm down, okay?
LARRY	I cannot do it. I will panic. We will go down.
Stewardess	All we need to know is that you're willing to assist passengers in the event of a non-traditional landing.
LARRY	I cannot be of any help whatsoever in any kind of non-traditional landing, or any traditional landing.

THE IMPROV PROCESS: SEASON FIVE

....
: This scene was improvised based on the following outline. :
....

Scene 15 from "The End" (Episode 10)
Larry pretends he's kosher.

THE OUTLINE

15. INT. SKI LODGE

Larry is trying to get some information from Cheryl about her sleeping arrangement. "What did you wear and where did he sleep?" They're interrupted by Rachel, who's demanding to know who put the toast with butter on her kosher plate? We then see her take the plate and bury it in a potted plant. Ben explains that she's purifying the plate. Larry, of course, concurs. He then quickly turns on Cheryl, admonishing her to be more careful.

WHAT WAS ON AIR

RACHEL	Good morning.
CHERYL	Good morning.
RACHEL	Um, were these not the plates we ate the pot roast on last night?
CHERYL	They are the same plates, but they've been washed and—
RACHEL	Uhm, I shouldn't be having dairy on these kind of plates. You know, as you know, the dairy and the meat are on two separate plates. That's a necessary rule of being Kosher. Where are the Milchig plates?
LARRY DAVID	What?
RACHEL	Where are they? Where are they?
LARRY DAVID	The Milchig plates? The Milchig plates. Well, they should be in the cabinet. You were told about the Milchig plates, were you not?
CHERYL	Okay. Well, I'm sorry about the, uh—
RACHEL	That's fine. I have to bury the plate and we'll be done with it.
CHERYL	You're gonna do what?
RACHEL	You have to bury the plate.
CHERYL	Why would you bury a plate?

LARRY DAVID	Why would you bury a plate? Tell her.
RACHEL	You have to bury the plate to purify it. It has to go underground.
LARRY DAVID (overlapping)	Purify, you have to purify it.
RACHEL	I'm sure you probably have a whole set of china in your backyard.
LARRY DAVID (overlapping)	Yeah.
CHERYL	Can't you just wash it and call it a day?
RACHEL	Uh, no, no we can't. Unless you want me to starve tonight.
LARRY DAVID (overlapping)	Nah, you bury. You bury. You bury. It's a little early for burying. I don't like to bury before coffee.
RACHEL	Do I smell bacon?
LARRY DAVID	Bacon?
CHERYL	Well—
LARRY DAVID	No, oh, I was a little gassy. I lit a match.

The End

CREDITS

THIS BOOK WAS PRODUCED BY

Melcher Media, Inc.
124 W. 13th Street
New York, NY 10011
www.melcher.com

DESIGN BY PH.D

Publisher .... *Charles Melcher*
Associate Publisher .... *Bonnie Eldon*
Editor in Chief .... *Duncan Bock*
Senior Editor .... *Lia Ronnen*
Assistant Editor .... *Lauren Nathan*
Production Director .... *Andrea Hirsh*

ACKNOWLEDGMENTS

Special thanks to Linda Balaban, Dort Clark, Larry David, Laura Fairchild, Tim Gibbons, Megan Murphy, Gavin Polone, Kate Simonides, and Robert Weide.

Thanks to Steve Adams, Cem Akin, Chris Albrecht, Tracey Barrett-Lee, David Brown, Sarah Condon, Bree Conover, Laurie David, Morty David, Laurie Epstein, Susie Essman, Jeff Garlin, Karina Gee, Jill Greenberg, Cheryl Hines, John Hughes, iocolor, Carolyn Joe, Nona Jones, David Kennerly, Rebecca Kennerly, Hilary Laffer, Candace Marks, Lauren Marino, Jada Miranda, David McAninch, Courteney F. Monroe, Richard Oren, Francesca Orsi, Jeffrey Peters, Clive Piercy, Holly Rothman, William Shinker, James Smith, Lindsey Stanberry, Carolyn Strauss, Shoshana Thaler, Winston Wesley, Megan Worman, and all the people who were interviewed for this book.

CURB YOUR ENTHUSIASM, SEASONS 1-5, AVAILABLE ON DVD FROM HBO VIDEO.

PHOTOGRAPHY CREDITS

All photos © HBO except for the following:
Endpapers: Jill Greenberg; pages 2-3: Jill Greenberg; page 4: Dort Clark; page 10, all photos courtesy of Larry David; page 13: courtesy of Morty David; page 29: Jill Greenberg; page 31: Jill Greenberg; page 40: courtesy of Larry David; page 41: Kenny Kramer; page 42: courtesy of Richard Lewis; page 45: courtesy of Morty David; page 49: courtesy of Steve Adams; page 53: Robert Weide; page 93: courtesy of Robert Weide/Whyaduck; page 100, left to right: courtesy of Larry David, courtesy of Morty David; page 103: courtesy of Morty David; page 106: David Kennerly/Getty Images; page 107: courtesy of Kenny Kramer; page 109: David Kennerly/Getty Images; pages 111-118: Dort Clark; page 123: Jill Greenberg; page 131: Jill Greenberg; page 137: Jill Greenberg; page 149: Alex Berliner, courtesy of Laurie David; page 157: Jill Greenberg; page 178-179: Map © Rand McNally, R.L. 06-S-53; page 180: courtesy of Susie Essman; page 191: Jill Greenberg; page 199: Jill Greenberg; page 203: Jill Greenberg; page 207: Jill Greenberg

RB YOUR ENTHUSIASM......THE PANTS TENT......TED AND MARY......PORNO GIL......THE BRACELET......INTERIOR DEC
CK OR TREAT......THE SHRIMP INCIDENT......THE THONG......THE ACUPUNCTURIST......THE DOLL......SHAQ......THE BAPT
RORIST ATTACK......THE SPECIAL SECTION......THE CORPSE-SNIFFING DOG......KRAZEE-EYEZ KILLA......MARY, JOSE